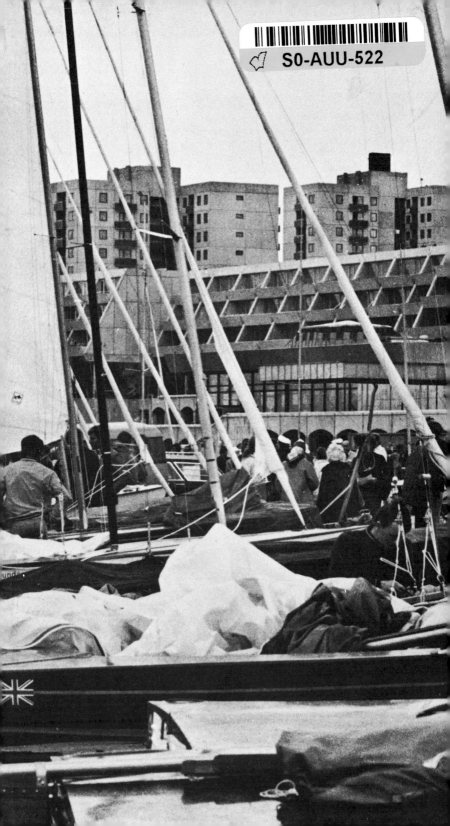

SAILING

SAILING

HUGH SOMERVILLE

THOMAS Y. CROWELL COMPANY
New York/Established 1834

Acknowledgments

The publishers are grateful to the following people who very kindly supplied the illustrations:

Beken of Cowes: 9, 15, 16t, 18, 40, 44t, 52b, 59, 66, 69b, 73; Camera Press: 44b, 55b, back endpapers; Camper & Nicholson: 52tr; J. Allan Cash: 83, (Eileen Ramsay), 36 colour, 38–9; Central Press: 57; Centrehurst Ltd: 81; Eastern Caribbean Tourist Boards: 75; Mary Evans Picture Library: 11, 14; Fox Photos: 27t, 41; German Embassy: front endpapers; Italian Tourist Office: 74; KH Publicity: 53r; Mansell Collection: 13b; Radio Times Hulton Picture Library: 49r; Richmond Marine: 23; Stanley Rosenfeld: 72; Syndication International: 45r colour; Royal Yachting Association: 55tL; E. Spalding: 21t, b colour, 27b; John Watney: 16b, 43, 48L, 55tr, 56t, 70, 78(2), 79(2); Yachting Monthly: 25, 53L, (Ian Gilchrist) 47, 66tr, 69t, 76, (Peter Warren) Half title page, (F. Armes) contents page; Yachts & Yachting: 48r, (Ed Lacey) 48L; Gordon Yeldham: 65 colour

The following people very kindly supplied plans for artists reference: Camper & Nicholson Ltd; The Fairey Aviation Co; Daily Mirror; Jack Holt Ltd; International Tornado Association; Richmond Marine Ltd; Snipe Class International Racing Association

L.C. Card 73–14097

Design by Paul Watkins & Florianne Henfield

Illustrations by Peter North and Suzanne Stevenson

Illustration Research by Susan Mayhew

First published 1974 by
Macmillan London Limited
London and Basingstoke
Associated companies in New York, Toronto, Dublin, Melbourne, Johannesburg and Madras

Phototypeset by Oliver Burridge Filmsetting Limited, Crawley, Sussex
Printed in Japan by Dai Nippon Printing Company

ISBN 0-690-00445-1

INTRODUCTION

King Charles II has always been given the credit for starting the sport of sailing in the British Isles. He was very fond of a small yacht given to him by the management of the East India Company. Her arrival on the Thames, in 1660, encouraged Commissioner Phineas Pett to build a boat during the following winter. A third was built by Christopher Pett, for the Duke of York, while a fourth yacht, built in Holland, was afloat in the Thames in 1661. The word 'yacht' is thought to have been derived from the Dutch 'Jachten', 'To Hunt', the Dutch being the real pioneers of sailing for pleasure.

There is a record of a race between the king and the Duke of York, in 1662, the course being from Greenwich to Gravesend and back and the stake being £100 ($250).

There is very little record of any further organized yachting in British waters until 1720, which was the date of the foundation of the Water Club of the Harbour of Cork in Ireland. The club had 25 members, who appear to have been content to cruise and to enjoy each other's convivial company. The club was very active until 1765, but then interest seems to have been lost. In 1806 another club was formed nearby at Little Monkstown. This appears to have been formed by the survivors of the old Water Club. It was called the Cork Yacht Club and later became the Royal Cork Yacht Club.

In the early nineteen sixties the Royal Cork was in grave danger of extinction, but in the season of 1966 it was amalgamated with the flourishing Royal Munster Yacht Club at Crosshaven, so that during the seasons of 1969 and 1970, it was able to celebrate its 250th anniversary. The celebrations in 1969 included a cruise in company along the South West Coast of Ireland, with yachts of the Cruising Club of America, the Royal Cruising Club and the Irish Cruising Club taking part.

Other very old clubs in the British Isles are the Lough Ree, formed in 1770, with a fine fleet of boats. In 1773 a 'Marine Fete' was held at Starcross, in Devon, and it is from this event that the Starcross Yacht Club, slightly dubiously, claims its origin. There is a record of a 'regatta', or 'Water party', being organized on Bassenthwaite, for the benefit of tourists, while there is also a record, in the shape of a cup in the Royal Thames Yacht Club, of a regatta at Whitstable, in 1792. It is doubtful, however, whether any of these events or organizations had any real influence on the growth of yachting, or sailing, as we know it nowadays.

It was in 1775 that the Cumberland Society was formed under the Royal patronage of Henry Frederick, Duke of Cumberland. By then there were a large number of small craft sailing on the Thames. In 1749, there had been a race from Greenwich to the Nore and back, for a plate presented by the Prince of Wales, but it was the Duke of Cumberland and the men he patronized, who really set British Yachting on the path which we know today.

Winthrop Alldrich, US Ambassador, remarked at a welcoming dinner at the Royal Thames Yacht Club, successor to the Cumberland Society, 'I find that the Royal Thames Yacht Club is older than the United States of America'.

It is recorded in *'Memorials of the Royal Yacht Squadron'* that: 'The primitive sport of yachting on the Thames was no sport of millionaires, like that of Cowes today (1903), but the relaxation of the professional man, who when his days work was done, stepped into his little cutter at the Temple Stairs, and of the retired city merchant with his country house at Chelsea or Marylebone and his boat on the river as the chief solace of his leisure'.

Much of the early racing took place between Blackfriars and Putney, and after it was over the competitors repaired to Mr

In the early nineteenth century Cowes on the Isle of Wight became a fashionable bathing resort for the English upper classes. The men soon became less interested in bathing and more interested in the local boats. Cowes was soon to become one of the most significant yachting centres in the world

Smith's Tea Gardens, at Vauxhall. Mr Smith was the first Commodore of the Cumberland Society and many of the early cups can be seen in the hall of the Royal Thames Yacht Club, together with a set of the Cumberland Fleet flags.

Thomas Taylor, who was Commodore of the Cumberland Society from 1780 until 1816, owned the centreboard cutter Cumberland, whose model is also in the Royal Thames, giving an idea of the type of boat in use at the time.

In 1823 the name of the Society was changed to H.M. Coronation Society, to mark the coronation of King George IV, but this only lasted a few months, because the Society was split in two over a protest in the very first race held under the new name. A number of members, who disagreed with the committee, held a meeting at the White Horse Tavern and formed the Thames Yacht Club, now the Royal Thames. The Society struggled on until it was dissolved in 1831. Most members joined the Thames Yacht Club, which has held a prominent position in British and international yachting ever since.

Meanwhile on the South Coast it was reported that: 'A taste for sea bathing among English people of condition', had attracted many such people to Cowes, on the Isle of Wight. There was a fine beach to the west of the castle, with bathing machines. The men, doubtless bored by the pleasures of the beach began to take an interest in sailing in the local craft. There was a race round the Isle of Wight as early as 1788. It was therefore inevitable that sooner or later these 'people of condition' should form a club. They did so at a meeting in 1815, at the Thatched House Tavern, St James's Street, London, calling it simply the Yacht Club, which is now the Royal Yacht Squadron.

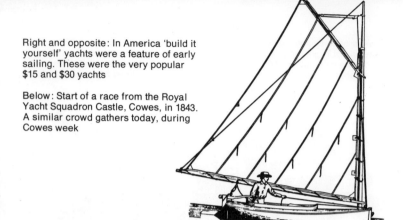

Right and opposite: In America 'build it yourself' yachts were a feature of early sailing. These were the very popular $15 and $30 yachts

Below: Start of a race from the Royal Yacht Squadron Castle, Cowes, in 1843. A similar crowd gathers today, during Cowes week

The senior yacht club of Scotland is the Royal Northern (1824), which for many years had an Irish branch, the same being true of the Royal Western Yacht Club of England, founded in 1827. It is the Royal Western which is host to the large international fleet which sails in the Fastnet race in alternate years to the race from Newport R.I. to Bermuda.

Many yacht clubs were formed in the British Commonwealth, the first of which was the Royal Gibraltar, the early members mostly consisting of army officers from the garrison. The oldest European club is the Royal Swedish Yacht Club (KSSS), while down in Australia the Royal Hobart Regatta Assocation claims its date of origin as 1838.

There is strong evidence of very early yachting in what became the United States of America, in colonial times. The first privately owned craft used for pleasure, and one of the first vessels ever built by white men in North America, was built in 1613 in New

Amsterdam by Adrian Block and his crew of Dutchmen. The yacht was called Onrust. In her they cruised along the coast exploring and found Block Island, named after the owner. During the 1700s, as the large estates were built up along Long Island Sound a few of the Dutch and later the English colonists built yachts. But it was not until the early 1800s that sailing became anything of an organized activity, although few had enough time or money to pursue it seriously .

The first large vessel built entirely for pleasure in America was Cleopatra's Barge, a hermaphrodite brig, owned by Captain George Crowninshield, and built in 1816. Taylor and Rosenfeld's *Story of American Yachting* records that Crowninshield died suddenly on board her in Salem harbour in 1817, after a cruise to the Mediterranean, and she became a cargo and packet vessel. She finally became King Kamehameha's royal yacht in the Hawaiian islands, where she was eventually wrecked.

As a celebration of Queen Victoria's Golden Jubilee a round-Britain yacht race was organised by the Royal Thames Yacht Club. This is an early engraving of the start which was at Southend

Opposite: In contrast, two modern offshore racers Prospect of Whitby and Warbaby beat down the Solent during Cowes Week 1972

When The New York Yacht Club was founded in 1844, by John C. Stevens on board his schooner Gimcrack, American yachts were beginning to assume a definite form. On both sides of the Atlantic yachts had originally been of the type following the local working craft, but in America at least there seemed to be a movement to improve performance.

It was Commodore Stevens and others who brought the schooner America to Britain, in 1851, the year of the Great Exhibition. They won the cup, which ever since has borne America's name, for winning a race round the Isle of Wight, in which they beat 15 of the best British yachts of the day. This cup is firmly bolted to the floor of the trophy room of the club, in West 44th Street, New York, despite 21 challenges for it, two from Canada, three from Australia. The America's Cup is the most publicized of all sailing trophies; indeed there are few sporting trophies of any kind which receive so much attention from the press of the world.

The reason for such massive publicity for the America's Cup is probably because, in the early days of the contests for it, there were few other sports reported in the newspapers. There may have been a bit of horse-racing and a prize fight or two, but neither baseball nor grid iron football had been organized by then. There was also the added attraction for the journalist of being able to report a defeat of the British. The reasons for the defeats can be seen in the magnificent model room of the New York Yacht Club. In this there are models of every challenger and defender displayed side by side. It does not require a very trained eye to discern that the defender, so far as design is concerned, has, with few exceptions, been superior to the challenger.

1 WHAT'S IT ALL ABOUT?

A few years ago, and perhaps even now to the unenlightened, sailing was regarded as a rich man's sport. The very mention of it tended to conjure up visions of pretentious looking people strutting about Cowes, or Newport RI, wearing white trousers and funny caps. In the early part of this century, the popular press frequently portrayed 'The big class', with Kings, Princes and millionaires sailing their graceful yachts, with the aid of large crews of professionals.

In those days there was practically no racing at Cowes at weekends, because the paid crews had to have rest, or maybe move the yacht to the next regatta round the coast. Even in the thirties the young 'gentleman' who wanted to take up sailing took the advice of Dixon Kemp, who in the early 1900s suggested that a boat of about 30ft waterline length, with two paid men, was the way to start.

In the USA, Canada, Australia and certainly New Zealand there was probably more of an accent on amateur or Corinthian sailing than there was in Britain, before Hitler's war. It was not until 1947 that there was regular yacht racing in the Solent on Sundays, while on the Clyde it was only in 1970 that the Sabbath was broken by the Royal Northern YC, the excuse being olympic training.

Nowadays in Britain more people actually sail on a summer weekend than play and watch the national game of cricket. In the

Opposite above: Gerard Lambert's
J class yacht Yankee, racing at Cowes
in 1935

Opposite below: A West Kirby Star
class boat in the Menai Straits regatta.
Designed near the turn of the century,
this class is still racing

USA, if they do not sail, the masses have discovered the motor boat, some eventually finding that sailing is more fun. It was in fact in the USA that there was more of a tendency for build-it-yourself craft. *The Story of American Yachting* shows many early craft for home building, a cult which in Britain was usually confined to the more worthy boys magazines.

The most famous of the 'build it yourself' boats, which became more truly International than many of the classes which have appeared since, was Wm. F. Crosby's creation, the Snipe. He is said to have returned from luncheon one day in New York, declaring to those in the offices of *The Rudder* magazine, that he was going to design: 'Something the b——s can build in their backyards'. For various reasons the Snipe never caught on in Britain, possibly because it was too big and heavy for British conditions but it was the strongest international dinghy class for many years. However there was something happening in Britain which was to revolutionize small boat racing.

Before 1936, when the National 12ft dinghy made its appearance, pushed along by the *Yachting World* magazine, there was only one class, the International 14 footer, which could be said to attract sailors from different parts of the country to race against each other. There were various quite numerous local dinghy classes, but these were usually confined to their particular district and their owners raced at their clubs, usually to the exclusion of going anywhere else.

There were some fine boats developed locally, some of which are still raced, such as the West Kirby Star, the Dublin Bay Waterwag and the Seaview 12ft dinghy. On the other side of the Atlantic there was still a great affection perhaps only in memory, for such craft as the Sandbagger, or the Cape Cod catboat, with more modern developments locally.

Annually, before 1939, Uffa Fox, who was a famous British designer and builder of racing dinghies, wrote five books, which have become yachting classics. In the war years, when sailing was difficult, if not impossible, many read them avidly and dreamed of the days when they could own a boat. Maybe they could never afford the beautiful boats of the international classes, which had not quite priced themselves out of existence by then, or the big offshore racers, which Uffa often described vividly. However, the dinghies, which were obviously his great love, were within financial reach and so, when war ended the big dinghy movement began.

The great feature of Uffa's boats was that they could plane. Their forward sections were of such a shape that as the boat gathered speed the wave tended to lift her, so that she skimmed along on her own bow wave. No one, least of all Uffa, would claim that he was the inventor of the planing hull, but in his boatbuilding apprenticeship he had built seaplane floats, so that he knew what

was happening. The contribution which Uffa made to modern sailing was in publicizing the joys of a light planing boat, and cashing in on it.

In 1945 Uffa was still going strong, having been involved with the development of an airborne lifeboat, which could be parachuted to airmen, who had ditched into the sea. Postwar restriction unfortunately soon damped his enthusiasm for building boats although he designed many good dinghies notably the Firefly. However, ready to take the stage was another designer, Jack Holt, who carried on the good work, and who, with his American partner, Beecher Moore, produced many of the very best dinghy classes which have appeared in postwar years. The secret of Jack's success was that most of his greatest designs were of boats which could be home built, following Crosby's Snipe. The fact that the majority of Holt dinghies were built by professionals matters very little. The chance was there for the man who wanted to build his own, without too many headaches, and in a reasonable enough time, before enthusiasm began to fade.

The *Yachting World* magazine had sponsored a design for a National 12, designed by Uffa Fox, called the Uffa King, which became something of a backbone to the class in the early days, as well as being the basis for many other designers, both amateur and professional to try to improve upon. It was the *Yachting World* which took Jack Holt in hand in 1945 with his original design for their Merlin class, which joined forces after a year or two with Ian Proctor's Rocket. Proctor himself is a prolific designer of small boats of all kinds, his most notable being The Tempest, a 20ft boat with a fixed keel, which made its debut as an olympic boat at Kiel, in 1972.

To return to Jack Holt, his GP 14, which is a handy family boat, as well as giving good racing, was one of *Yachting World's* earliest 'do-it-yourself' dinghies, following the Cadet, which was designed as a boat for children to learn to race. Then came the Hornet, a really exciting boat. The *News Chronicle* of London, of sad memory, commissioned Jack to design the Enterprise, which, with the Cadet, is officially recognized as International, by the world ruling body of the sport, the International Yacht Racing Union. Of all the boats designed by Jack Holt, the one which really sold like hotcakes, was the Mirror dinghy, sponsored by the London *Daily Mirror*. With 'do-it-yourself' expert Barry Bucknall helping with constructional details, this boat was a winner from the start and has been built and sailed by youngsters of all ages, in very many countries.

Some may well ask, 'What do these boats cost?' This book was written as the dollar was devalued and the pound sterling floated, so that any figure given could be inaccurate. Some of the classes mentioned can now be supplied with a glass fibre hull, which will probably cost more than timber or plywood although maintenance

Children sailing Optimist pram dinghies.
This class originated in Florida, but
spread rapidly through Europe,
principally in Scandinavia

will be less. Suffice to say that most compare in cost *new*, with a secondhand or used motor car, with the International 14 ranking with the more aristocratic.

Unless you live by the sea, an essential part of the 'outfit', to borrow a word from the motorboat racing fraternity, is a road trailer. This gives mobility, so that the boat can be kept at home if you have space, so that you are saved storage in a club dinghy park, or boat shed. You can also attend to small details, which very often require more time than anything else, and you have the satisfaction of knowing that the job has been done by you yourself. You can also take the boat away for holidays, or to open dinghy meetings which are so much a part of the dinghy scene.

Over the years, in the dinghy world, a remarkable spirit of reciprocation of hospitality has grown up. Those from a club in the south may have made friends with those in the north. These friendships frequently grow, so that one couple may offer hospitality at 'A' while, when they visit 'B', they find they are welcome. This happy atmosphere extends to friends from overseas. This can save hotel bills or the chore of camping. Most big dinghy meetings are organized by those who recognize the need for reasonably priced accommodation and cater for this, and also for camping sites and caravan parks. Over the years something of a myth has been built up, with dinghy sailors pleading extreme poverty at all times. Naturally some are younger or just not so well off as others, but many will go on sailing dinghies until they are too infirm to climb aboard. I know one intrepid lady who went on strike, so far as crewing in her husband's dinghy was concerned. It was the day she first drew the old age pension! So far as poverty is concerned, next time a reader finds himself at one of the big dinghy clubs, maybe at the Midwinter series, or in Chichester Harbour, or at one of the big reservoirs in the English Midlands, a few minutes in the car park could be revealing. Maybe the cars belong to the users' firms. Many of them must be employed by or even own some very rich firms.

Bigger boats have not been mentioned, simply because in the evolution of modern British sailing there was little progress in the development of the small cruising yacht until about the middle or late fifties. The newcomers to sailing mostly started in dinghies anyway and probably had not yet graduated to their expensive cars. Those already converted prewar, and in the USA, kept mainly to prewar ideas. Anyway there was not really very much money in Britain until the Stock Exchange boom of 1959, to spend on bigger boats, for those who felt they had enough of the discomfort of dinghy sailing.

Most sailors agree that it is best to start to learn sailing in a dinghy, where the quick reactions necessary to avoid minor or major disaster, will require a novice to be on his mettle. I know of only one really successful international racing yachtsman, who

Right: The Mirror Dinghy was
introduced by the English daily
newspaper. Designed by Jack Holt and
Barry Bucknell, there are now 40,000 of
them.

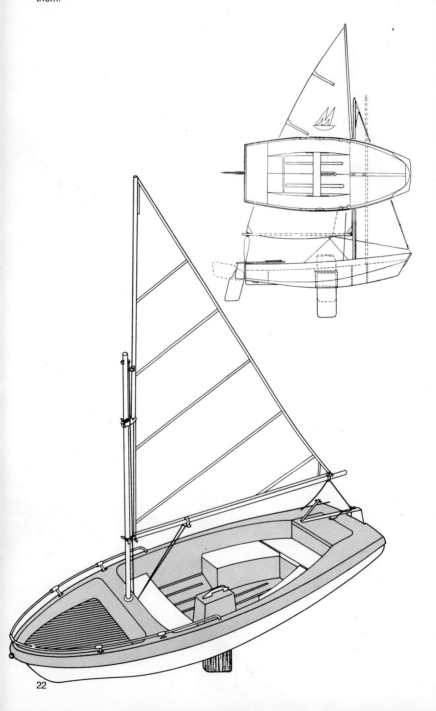

Opposite below and below: the Skipper
dinghy, available in 12ft and 14ft
versions. Designed by Peter Milne as a
family dinghy it is an excellent
beginner's boat

did not start in a dinghy. He had to 'rough it' in his father's 200-ton schooner!

There are some who wish to sail, but are not, and never will be, the slightest bit interested in racing. They may wish to belong to a yacht club for convenience sake, but shy like startled gazelles at the sight of the racing 'hearties' gathered round the club bar, telling each other for the umpteenth time how they did it, or didn't.

In recent years several firms have evolved a form of small cruising yacht. Many of these craft, such as those designed by Westerly Marine, of Waterlooville, England, and Pearson's of Bristol R.I., USA, are not designed for great speed under sail, but are safe and comfortable. Obviously such boats vary in price, but a rough guide is that one should not think of buying a boat costing more than one's yearly income but other commitments may be relevant. Some may have plenty of capital, so good luck to them, but whatever their financial state, take care that the family will agree to this step.

It is possible to raise a mortgage on a yacht, provided she is registered at the local Customs house. Apart from the convenience of being able to mortgage one's yacht, the fact that she is registered means that title can be proved quite simply. The registered owner will be given a Certificate of Registry, which is an impressive document with a copy of the registered details of the vessel, which has all the rights and privileges of a real proper Ship. This helps when going abroad, and returning from a foreign port. I know of a friend who returned to England from France in an unregistered yacht, which had been built abroad. He had to leave his boat in the care of the Customs at his port of arrival, to go to London to get proof, from the broker who had supplied the boat, that Customs duty had been paid on her.

In Britain and the Commonwealth another advantage of having a yacht registered is part of the ritual of the sport. If the owner is a member of a yacht club, which has been granted the privilege of wearing a special ensign, ie Blue, or defaced Red, he can on obtaining a warrant from the Admiralty, wear his ensign.

Obviously a novice who wants to buy a boat should take advice about the vessel he wants to buy. No one in their senses would buy a house without a survey, so why a boat, even the smallest? For a dinghy the advice of a local boatbuilder or an expert on her class will probably suffice. For a bigger boat a qualified surveyor is required. Several of these advertize in the yachting press. If the yacht is built under a classification by Lloyds Register, eg 100A1 (which means that with Lloyds supervision she should last 100 years or so) they will survey her for you. The cost of a survey is the responsibility of the would be purchaser and there were, in the days before glass fibre yachts, many purchasers who rued the day that they bought a yacht without a proper survey. Even in this day of plastic boats a survey is worthwhile.

A typical holiday weekend, with four types of dinghy, GP 14, Enterprise, Heron and Merlin/Rocket, at Morfa Bychen, North Wales

So you want to begin?

Having attempted to give some idea of the structure of the modern sailing world, which will be dealt with in greater detail in the next chapter, the layman may well ask a couple of questions. The first is: 'Is sailing dangerous?' The second: 'Is sailing a cinch?'

The simple answer to the first is: 'Yes, it can be.' It is possible that the dangers of sailing have been greatly exaggerated in sections of the press, due to propaganda by various bodies, who either want to publicize themselves, or by certain bodies who view sailing, and control of it, as a possible future source of revenue. Once statutory control goes onto any form of activity it produces some form of taxation, which never comes off, although names of taxes sometimes change. In America, control of pleasure craft is a reality and not a very happy one, although the US Coastguard do much to help yachtsmen.

The ruling body of the sport in Britain is the Royal Yachting Association. They have been tireless in their efforts to keep sailing from statutory controls, persuading government departments that voluntary control of the sport through education and well organized training programmes, through clubs and sailing schools, is best for all concerned. It is therefore up to newcomers to the sport in Britain to try to become as proficient as possible, if only to avoid what has happened in the USA.

In sailing one is competing with the elements, the wind and
weather and the sea. These are uncompromising, so that only
common sense on the part of the owner of a boat, and his crew,
can prevent accidents. Even so they may be unlucky. Several very
experienced sailors have been known to get into trouble, sometimes through bad luck, but very often because of a lack of vigil-
ance. The wind and the sea will sometimes frighten you, so that
the only answer is to see that you do not lack knowledge. You must
also ensure that your boat is as well found in all respects as it
possibly can be. If you cannot afford something which will make
your boat safer, you should think seriously whether you can afford
that boat at all. In the Lloyds marine insurance policies the owner
is described as: 'Master under God'. It is worth remembering.

Sailing is not a cinch. There have, over the years, been some
very funny books and articles published on amusing incidents
afloat. Take these for what they are worth. You may not get away
with it. Once you have started sailing you should never stop
learning. If indeed you ever think you know it all, it is time you
packed up, because you will just be a menace.

Sailing is a sport which can be taken up at almost any age.
There is, however, a tendency on the part of some sailing-mad
parents to start their children much too young. The child could
be scared stiff at the age of five, but, had he or she been left alone,
might have taken to the water later.

Before being allowed to sail in a dinghy, a child should be able
to swim, and many clubs sensibly insist that children should wear
lifejackets when sailing. In a bigger boat the lifebelts for children
rule should certainly be enforced.

There are only two kinds of women in boats, the seaworthy and
the unseaworthy. The seaworthy really enjoy it and are simply
wonderful. There are some who will tolerate it because their mate
likes it, but sooner or later the showdown will come. It was for this
reason that I gave the word of warning about the potential cruising
boat owner. The owner may find himself having to sell it and buy
the country cottage for the wife after all.

How do I start learning?

This is a question frequently asked by those who may have visited
boat shows, or maybe seen people appearing to enjoy themselves
in sailing boats on the water. The answer first of all could be:
'Have you any friends who sail?'

If this is so, they may be able to help, if only to introduce you to a
group, in a club probably, who have the same background as
yourself. Remember that you are going to start sailing as a means
of spending your leisure, so it is best to start with friends, if this is
possible. There are clubs which encourage the training of beginners, although this aspect is probably taken more seriously in the
USA than it is in Britain.

There are clubs on both sides of the Atlantic, as well as other parts of the world where sailing is a recreation, which have junior sections, where every effort is made to teach the young. However, there is sometimes a gap, when it comes to those who wish to take up sailing when grown up, or even in middle age. For such people there are Sailing Schools, where, for a fee, they can take a short course, in order to learn the rudiments. Many of these schools also hold children's classes during the school vacations.

A very particular type of school-cum-club, has grown up recently in Europe in the shape of the International Sailing School at Glenans, in France; another example of this type of operation being the Island Cruising Club, of Salcombe, England. In both of these, while the club provides the basic facilities, including boats of all sizes, and a few paid instructors, the members themselves play a very considerable part in training the uninitiated, and in fitting out and maintaining the boats.

You cannot learn how to sail a boat from a book, but you can, if you find a good book on the rudiments, at least gain some idea of what the whole business is all about. Some titles for the beginner are given on page 89. Before going for one's very first sail it is worthwhile studying some of the jargon involved. There are some who tend to regard this as ridiculous, but, after all, if one is taking up any game or sport, it is worth studying the rules, even if you are going to watch. A young lady from a well known Boston yachting family once completely ruined a romance with one of Britain's leading sailors, by referring to her possible future parents-in-law's pack of Foxhounds as: 'Them there li'l dawgs'.

There are some who have sailed all their lives and who have never learned to swim. They may have been very lucky. I have already mentioned that no child should be allowed to start sailing until he or she is a proficient swimmer. They will probably live to regret it in later life if they have not learned to swim in any case. It is also helpful if the trainee sailor can at least row a dinghy. In these days of racing type dinghies this is sometimes overlooked.

There are many books on knots, splices, bends and hitches, and while the art of making fancy knots is a fascinating subject in itself and excellent for occupying children afloat on a wet day, the beginner should at least know how to tie a reef knot, a clove hitch and bowline, before setting out for his first sail (opposite). Even better he should be able to tie them behind his back and in the dark.

The drawings on pages 30, 31 and 33 give the points of sailing and on pages 32, 34 and 35 the basic parts and rigs of a boat. The beginner should appreciate the difference between a keel-boat which should not capsize, and a dinghy in which this is possible.

Before the first sail

Maybe you have been invited, or have arranged to go for your very first sail. Here are some simple things to remember:

It is essential to know a few basic
knots before going sailing: 1 Reef Knot
2 Bowline 3 Clove Hitch

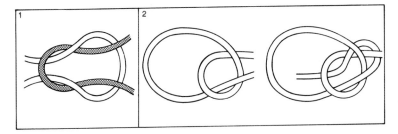

1 *Be sure that you arrive at the appointed time* Apart from bad manners, there may be other considerations which may have been vital should you arrive late. For instance, the tide may turn, the wind may drop, or strengthen, or your skipper may have had some master plan which you have sabotaged. Punctuality is therefore essential.

2 *Be properly dressed for sailing* Before going, ask your skipper what he expects you to wear. The first essential is non slip shoes. There are plenty of these of all types on the market and they need not cost much. He may be able to advise you on foul weather gear, or even be able to lend you some. If it is cold, make sure that you have enough warm clothing, before putting on foul weather gear. An extra jersey never did anyone any harm. Remember that it is better to be warm and wet than cold and wet. The wet suit is one of the greatest advances in sailing clothing for cold climates.

If your first sail is in tropical waters, remember to keep well covered from the effects of the sun. In a small boat you will not be moving about very much, so that exposed extremities, such as bare knees and tops of feet, can become very sore.

3 *Carry a knife and a spike* These, or a combination of the two, should be carried where they can be found quickly in an emergency. They are not much good buried under a few layers of clothing.

4 *Lifebelts may be obligatory* They should be for children in any case, but in some waters, such as English reservoirs they must be worn as a condition for the club to be allowed to use the water. Ask the skipper if in doubt.

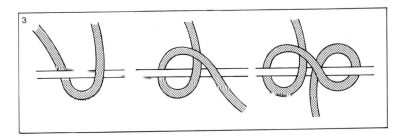

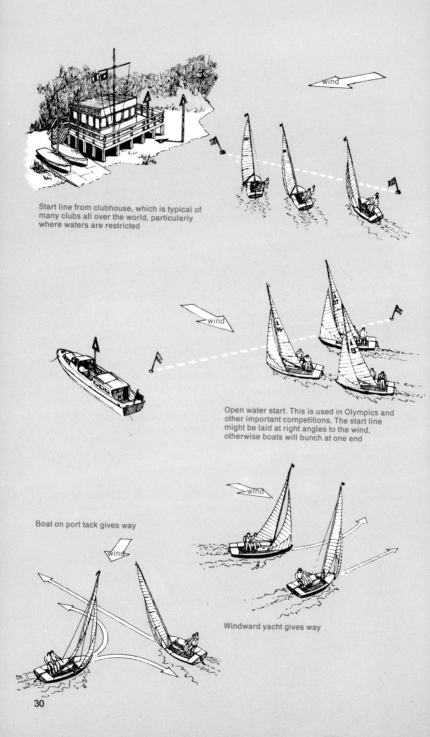

Start line from clubhouse, which is typical of many clubs all over the world, particularly where waters are restricted

Open water start. This is used in Olympics and other important competitions. The start line might be laid at right angles to the wind, otherwise boats will bunch at one end

Boat on port tack gives way

Windward yacht gives way

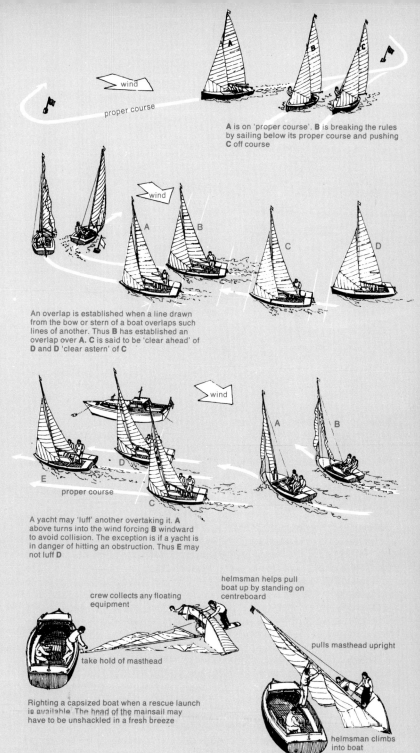

A is on 'proper course'. B is breaking the rules by sailing below its proper course and pushing C off course

An overlap is established when a line drawn from the bow or stern of a boat overlaps such lines of another. Thus B has established an overlap over A. C is said to be 'clear ahead' of D and D 'clear astern' of C

A yacht may 'luff' another overtaking it. A above turns into the wind forcing B windward to avoid collision. The exception is if a yacht is in danger of hitting an obstruction. Thus E may not luff D

crew collects any floating equipment

take hold of masthead

helmsman helps pull boat up by standing on centreboard

pulls masthead upright

helmsman climbs into boat

Righting a capsized boat when a rescue launch is available. The head of the mainsail may have to be unshackled in a fresh breeze

5 *Rings and watchstraps can be dangerous* They may get caught up, so find somewhere safe to leave them, ashore for preference. I once had the delicious pleasure of extricating a young actress, whose charm bracelet had caught in a jib sheet block. While a few hundred pound sterling or dollars worth of Cartier or Tiffany's best were saved from a watery grave, this could have been very dangerous for her.

6 *Offer to help* You may find the process of rigging the boat bewilderingly complicated and feel out of place. If your skipper does not give you a simple task to start with, watch what the others do, so that you can be of some use next time, and maybe you will be able to help with putting the boat to bed.

If the boat is a dinghy your main job will almost certainly be to help keep the boat upright. To do this you will have to sit on the windward side. That is the side from which the wind is blowing. The sheltered side is the lee side, an expression you will probably have heard before. Do not sit to leeward in a dinghy unless your skipper tells you to do so.

There are one or two more rules to remember, if your introduction to sailing is to be in a habitable yacht.

1 *Do not arrive with stiff luggage* Your gear will have to be stowed in a minute space, perhaps a locker only a foot or two long and a few inches deep, so make everything as compact as possible. Many yacht chandlers supply soft bags, made by sailmakers, for sailing clothing. These are useful for any sporting activity, so get one. They will not take up space when empty.

Left: A typical dinghy

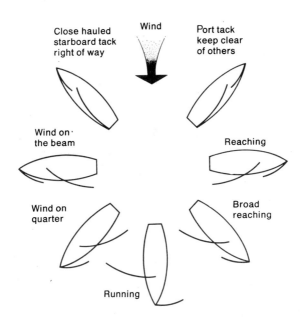

Close hauled
starboard tack
right of way

Wind

Port tack
keep clear
of others

Wind on
the beam

Reaching

Wind on
quarter

Broad
reaching

Running

2 *Find out how the lavatory works* There are different makes of these, so be sure that you can work the one you are to be ship-mates with, and *don't block it* by throwing match sticks and the like into it.

3 *Never stand in hatchways* You can see what I mean from the photograph on page 36. You must let people pass, and may find yourself unpopular if you stand in the way of the skipper. It does no harm to keep your head down, but still take an intelligent interest in what is going on.

A general word of warning

You may be going on this your very first sail with an old friend. He may be the mildest of men ashore, kind to animals, good to children, never beats his wife, etc. However, now that he is in charge of his yacht, he may be suffering the 'loneliness of com-mand'. He will have assumed the responsibility of taking you and maybe others sailing, and trying to get himself home alive too. In the process there may be some change of character. His second name may turn out to be Bligh. If he shouts or swears at you, *he probably does not mean it*. If you can't stand it, despite your friendship ashore, try another skipper. Better still learn enough about it all to be able to take charge of your own boat, as quickly as possible. Above all do not chatter, when the skipper has an anxious look on his face, and do not answer back when he tells you to do something in a sharpish tone of voice. He probably wants action—quick.

Old fashioned rigs for dinghies. Left to right:
Standing lug, Balanced lug, Gunter

Left to right: Spritsail rig, Gaff rig, and
Bermudan. A few dinghies have a spritsail rig,
notably the Optimist. Most are now Bermudan

Parts of a jib, Bermudan, and gaff mainsail

Typical ketch rig of many British fishing boats
of the days of sail

Jib headed   Gaff headed   Yard headed
Types of rig of fore and aft rigged craft

This schooner has a gaff headed foresail and
jib headed main

34

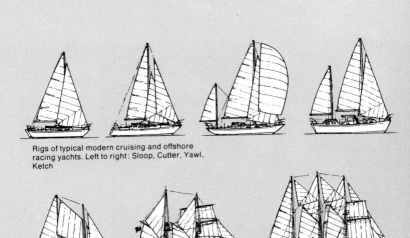

Rigs of typical modern cruising and offshore racing yachts. Left to right: Sloop, Cutter, Yawl, Ketch

Schooner

Topsail schooner

Three masted topsail schooner

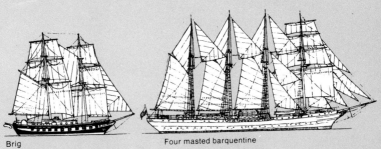

Brig

Four masted barquentine

Barque – three masted

Full-rigged ship

2 ASPECTS OF SAILING

The Offshore racer Roundabout, off
Cowes. Designed for the One Ton Cup,
she has been a serious competitor at
Cowes for many years

Having tried in the last chapter to give some reasons why sailing nowadays can be within the financial reach of most people, I may contradict this by showing how various aspects of sailing have developed. In the course of this development, it has been inevitable that some branches of the sport have become incredibly expensive, although those who have the best interests of sailors at heart have always tried to make the sport cheaper. Sometimes, too, classes have just died, because they have become too expensive, so that potential owners just do not want that type of boat.

Roughly speaking there are two types of sailor. The racing man and the cruising man. Racing appeals to the highly competitive, while cruising catches the man who prefers to relax and maybe explore the district in which he may keep his boat, or perhaps he will go further afield. The cruising man may even feel so strongly about racing that he will tend to regard the racing man as a form of maritime road-hog, who ruins the sport by being over competitive.

Racing

In the last chapter the difference was explained between dinghy and keel boat. Now we can consider the difference between One-design and Restricted classes. Many classes have appeared which are one-design. In other words, subject sometimes to various restrictions, the boats are all the same. There are varying types of One-design classes. Some have very strict rules, a case being the International OD's, produced by Norwegian designer Bjarne Aas, which were only built by him, and which had very strict rules about such things as permitted fittings, choice of sail-maker and even a restriction on how often one might buy replacement sails. All this made for even competition and kept costs down as much as possible, although the International has become an expensive boat by modern standards.

There are One-design classes that have looser rules. They also permit certain differences within the general framework of these rules. For instance the Dragon and Star classes have fairly open rules in some aspects. They can be built anywhere, although naturally there are builders who are in fashion because they produce winners. However, there is some scope for the ingenious in trying to produce new ways of making their boats go faster, although it can be said that such 'go fast' thought tends to swing round and round periodically, so that the latest thinking of the present day, may have become unfashionable ten years ago, or maybe more. Any student of yacht racing should, if he is trying to improve performance, at least look back into the history of his class to see what has been tried before. He may easily find that he would be well advised to try something that had been usual practice a few years ago, modifying it to modern requirements.

Take for example a gadget, which has now become almost universal in modern racing dinghies—the 'self bailer'. This is designed to extract water from a dinghy while it is sailing. About fifteen years ago these gadgets were being fitted to dinghies, some models being somewhat crude and inefficient. It was in 1958 that a team of dinghy sailors appeared in Cowes, having brought their International 14ft dinghies from New Zealand. They astonished everyone by the simplicity of their self bailers, which were copied from those used by the Chinese in their sampans for centuries!

Measurement rules

The earliest yachts almost certainly raced level, with the first boat home winning the prize. There is a record of a race between King Charles II and the Duke of York, in 1662, for a stake of £100 ($250), from Greenwich to Gravesend. However, yachtsmen were not long in trying to introduce rules of measurement, so that yachts could race level, or if they did not, they could at least be handicapped. There is record of a 'builders' or 'yacht measurement' rule of 1770, but perhaps the best known of the rules which were evolved, was that which many clubs, including the R. Thames YC adopted in 1854 and which is still known as Thames measurement. The formula for this is:

$$\frac{L-B \times B \times \frac{1}{2}B}{94} = \text{tonnage}$$

This is still used for estimating tonnage and until very recently for quoting prices in the British Isles. In this formula B is the extreme beam, or breadth, while L is the length between the bow

The Dragon Class racing off Abersoch, North Wales. The Dragon was an Olympic class from 1948 until 1972, but has been dropped for the 1976 Olympics on the grounds of expense

and the stern post on deck. This formula penalizes beam and is one of the causes of the narrowness of British yachts, compared to those from the USA.

Two other formulas were tried in Britain before the introduction of the 'International Rule of 1906'. This was the result of correspondence between Major Brooke Heckstall-Smith, secretary of the Yacht Racing Association and the YC de France. They decided to call a conference to devize an international measurement rule. Eleven countries met in 1906 and formed what is now the International Yacht Racing Union.

Their measurement formula has produced some very fine racing yachts, known as the 'Metre boats'. The formula is that used for the building of the 12 metres which currently race for the America's Cup. This formula is:

$$\frac{L+2d+\sqrt{S-F}}{2.37} = \text{rating}$$

L is measured length
d is 'girth difference' (ie the difference between the girth measured along the skin and the girth measured by a stretched chain)
S is measured sail area, which is that of the mainsail plus 85 per cent of the foretriangle.
F is freeboard.

Meanwhile on the other side of the Atlantic they had evolved the Universal Rule, under which, among other fine yachts, the 'J' class were built. After the first world war it was agreed that while the Americans would adopt the International Rule for yachts of 12 metres and less, Europe would adopt the Universal rule for

39

bigger yachts. The America's Cup races of 1930, 1934 and 1937 were sailed in 'J' class yachts, which died out as a class after the last of those contests due to rising costs.

The last of the IYRU measurement rules to appear, was that under which the 5.5 metre class are built. This was almost the same as an old formula of 1920. The 5.5 metres have limited appeal, partly because of cost. That is why they were dropped from the Olympic Games after the 1968 regatta.

Looking at the foregoing, it is quite easy to appreciate that a pattern was emerging in the sailing world, so far as racing was concerned. Before World War I, there was much handicap racing amongst big boats, with One designs, both dinghy and keel boat beginning to make their presence felt by the 1890s.

After World War I the 'twenties and 'thirties was the heyday of the Metre boats, with one design racing making a very strong challenge and, as already mentioned in Chapter 1, the dinghies knocking at the door.

Came the end of World War II, the Metre boats still had a bit of life, but rising costs were making new building very expensive. The dinghy boom really had begun, while the Offshore Racing cult, which had started slowly through the efforts of enthusiasts

on both sides of the Atlantic, was also beginning to gain strength. In the last decade it has grown to be a really great force in the modern sailing scene.

Offshore racing

The United States of America led the world by introducing offshore racing in comparatively small yachts. The famous transatlantic race of 1905 attracted eleven boats from three countries: the USA, Britain and Germany. The winner, the three masted schooner Atlantic, sailed the 3,014 mile course from Sandy Hook to the Lizard, in 12 days 4 hours, which has not been beaten.

The first Bermuda race was organized by Thomas Fleming Day, then editor of *Rudder*, the oldest surviving yachting magazine. There were three entries. On the American West coast the big Trans-pacific race, from California to Hawaii was first sailed in 1906, the same year as the first Bermuda.

Older than either the Bermuda or Transpac races, is the Mackinac race run by the Chicago YC. This was first sailed in 1898.

Compared with these events, the Fastnet race, inaugurated in 1925, when the Royal Ocean Racing Club was born, is quite a youngster. Even younger is the Sydney-Hobart which was instigated by Capt John H. Illingworth in 1945.

Probably the contest which has done most to help the development of international competition in Offshore racing is the Admiral's Cup. In this teams of three yachts from as many as 16 countries race each other within the framework of four races, the Fastnet (605 miles), the Channel Race (200 miles) and two special races held during Cowes Regatta. Points are awarded with a weighting of three points for the Fastnet, two for Channel and one for each boat beaten, in the two inshore races. The holder, who won the last of these contests, held in alternate years to the Bermuda race, is Britain, the team being led to victory in 1971 by Prime Minister Edward Heath.

Naturally the Admiral's Cup has its imitators, with the Onion Patch trophy competition held with the Bermuda Race as its climax, and the Southern Cross Trophy, with the finish in the Sydney–Hobart.

One of the most enjoyable offshore racing gatherings is always the US Southern Ocean Racing Conference series, known as the Southern circuit. Originally the big race of this was the St Petersburg–Havana, but this came to an end with the Castro regime's take-over. Since then the big race has been the 403 mile St Peterburg–Fort Lauderdale, which is hailed as Florida's answer to the Fastnet. It can be just as tough, although once into the Gulf Stream outside the Florida Keys, at least the water is warm. The other big race in the Southern circuit is the highly enjoyable Miami–Nassau, following a dog leg course, which can provide problems, starting as it does with a 57-mile dash across the Gulf Stream. No doubt as the cult of offshore racing gains greater strength, we shall see offshore men from all over the world making this an annual affair, as do the sailors from the Great Lakes and the North Eastern seaboard of the USA.

For very many years the offshore racing world was divided between those who raced under the rating rule of the Cruising Club of America, and those of the rest of the world who followed the Royal Ocean Racing Club.

Now, since the beginning of 1971 the two sides of the world are united in a common rule, the International Offshore Rating rule, the one in force in 1973 being called IOR Mk III for short. While this rule, which is mainly the brain child of that very great designer Olin Stephens, is not perfect and has been shown to have a loophole or two, it has at least brought the world together under a common formula. No longer therefore do American yachtsmen have an excuse that their boats did not fare well in the Fastnet because it was under the unfamiliar RORC rule, or vice versa. A British crew even won the 1972 Bermuda race, which no British sailors had ever done before. Albeit they won with a boat designed by an American, Olin Stephens, and built in Finland!

World girdling and the 'stunt' races

At the time of reading this book there may be more than a hundred small yachts struggling round the world. Some may be in fine shape, with the craft maintained regardless of expense, while others may be kept on a 'shoe string'. In some the owners may be fulfilling a life's ambition to escape from it all, having made enough money to do so, while others may feel that this is their big chance to make a name for themselves. Maybe they can do something which nobody else has achieved.

The man who tends to be blamed for this ocean voyaging habit is Captain Joshua Slocum. He started his famous round-the-world voyage in the 37ft sloop, Spray leaving Boston 24 April 1895. He sailed singlehanded, and is said to have helped to defray his expenses by selling some Tallow, which he had found floating off Cape Horn, in Australia, to a soapmaker.

Below: The giant trimaran Pen Duick IV, in which Alain Colas won the *Observer* Single-handed Transatlantic Race in 1972

Bottom: Suhaili, in which Robin Knox-Johnston won the Single-handed round-the-World Race organized by the *Sunday Times*. He was the first man to sail single-handed round the world non-stop

Sir Francis Chichester setting sail from
Sydney in Gipsy Moth IV in 1967

As he was one of the first of such voyagers to get himself any publicity, his *Sailing Alone Round the World* was one of the few of the 'world girdler's books' which made much more than the publisher's advance, until modern times. Slocum was also a good photographer and one of the pioneers of the illustrated sailing lecture.

Perhaps the ultimate idea in the 'world girdling' habit was reached when, in 1960, there was the first Single-handed Transatlantic Race, which was the brain child of Lt-Col. H. G. Hasler. In this four yachts took part, the winner being Sir Francis Chichester's Gipsy Moth III, which took $40\frac{1}{2}$ days from Plymouth to New York. Chichester followed this by sailing across the Atlantic again in 1962, taking 33 days 15 hours, but then came his famous voyage round the world, stopping only at Sydney, in Gipsy Moth IV. He sailed from Plymouth to Sydney in 107 days, and back to Plymouth in 119, making the longest passage by a small vessel without a port of call of 15,500 miles, although this was soon to be beaten several times.

Perhaps as a result of Chichester's voyage, the London *Sunday Times*, who had sponsored him, again sponsored a stunt, of a race single-handed round-the-world non-stop. This was won by Robin Knox Johnston in Suhaili, in which he had already sailed across oceans, from Bombay to London. The only thing left appeared to be for someone to sail round the world single-handed round-the-world non-stop against the prevailing westerly winds, the opposite direction to Knox Johnston. This was achieved by Sergeant Chay Blyth, in British Steel, who arrived back from this epic during Cowes Week of 1971.

The Single-handed Transatlantic still continues as a race at four year intervals. A round-the-world race for Offshore racing type yachts was scheduled to start in Autumn 1973, organized by the Royal Naval Sailing Association and sponsored by Whitbread's brewery. Another race from London to Sydney, via Cape of Good Hope and back via Cape Horn, will be sailed in 1975, with the blessing of the Royal Ocean Racing Club, whose jubilee year it is, and the Royal Thames YC who celebrate the 200th birthday of their forerunner, the Cumberland Fleet. Whether or not these great stunts, with fully crewed offshore racers taking part, will benefit the sport, remains to be seen.

Certainly the Single-handed Transatlantic Race, at least, has helped to publicize and to aid development of multi-hulled craft, whose performance offshore has long been suspect in the eyes of those who sail conventional single-hulled craft. There will always be sailing men, who possess enough originality of thought to try something new. Many of those who go sailing wish they could break out in some way, but family or business ties prevent them from doing anything but sail with their families at weekends and perhaps an extended cruise at holiday time.

3 THE MEN WHO SAIL

As already mentioned in previous chapters, those who sail do so for various reasons. They may be stimulated by the competitive side of sailing. They may like the peace and solitude which can be found on the water, or they may want to 'prove themselves' in various ways, usually by long voyages, probably quite alone.

The racing men obviously receive more publicity than those who cruise, but there is no doubt that the voyages of Sir Francis Chichester are the exception to this general rule. They, sponsored as they were by national newspapers, brought sailing to the notice of the man-in-the-street. Another, who, by taking up sailing, and more recently offshore racing, has given the sport a great boost, is Edward Heath.

There is an excellent publication, *Who's Who in Yachting*, published four years ago and it is to be hoped that this will be brought up to date from time to time. While there is not enough space in a mere chapter to give the names of a fraction of those whose names are well known in the yachting world, here are a few, who have either distinguished themselves in the past, or are currently at the top. We start with:

The racing men
Amongst racing men the world over there is one who has the distinction of winning four Olympic Gold medals in a row. He is Paul Bert Elvström, who was born in 1928, and is now a successful sailmaker and boatbuilder. His gold medals were won in the Firefly class in 1948 and in the Finn, in 1952, 1956 and 1960. As well as this he has won the World Championship of the Finn, 5.5 metre, Star, 505, Snipe and Soling classes, as well as winning other regional championships.

With the growing interest in sailing and the slightly out-of-date attitude of many of those involved with the Olympic Games, there is a very thin dividing line between the amateur and professional, so far as Olympics are concerned. This is not so narrow for IYRU, the world governing body of yachting requirements, because without sailmakers and boatbuilders actually competing, there would be precious little progress in the sport. If successful sailors did not write about it, again there would be no guide to the beginner. However, in view of the attitude of some Olympic officials, particularly after the Winter Olympics, some successful sailors found themselves under severe scrutiny before the 1972 regatta at Kiel, in view of their commercial interests. Elvström in particular suffered severe strain.

Another who bids fair to be in the sailing limelight for many years to come is Rodney Pattisson, born 1943, who retired from the Royal Navy just before the 1972 Olympics. At that regatta, sailing his Flying Dutchman, he won his second Gold medal, repeating his outstanding success of 1968. In the latter regatta he finished first six times out of seven, although he was disqualified for an instant in the opening race. Lesser men would have been discouraged by such a misfortune, but the fact that he was not, only underlines the courage of the man.

Apart from his Olympic successes, Pattisson won every major Flying Dutchman title for which he entered between these two Olympiads, in fact was hardly ever beaten at all. Since retiring from the navy he has been a director of a boatbuilding firm.

Turning across the Atlantic there are two sailors who have been thorns in the sides of those who have tried to take the America's Cup. The first is the late Harold S. Vanderbilt, who was helmsman

and part or full owner of three defenders, Enterprise, Rainbow and Ranger. He was also, although advancing in years, very much the *eminence grise* behind most of the postwar cup defenders. Another contribution by Mr Vanderbilt to the yachting fraternity, was the code of racing rules which he introduced to the North American Yacht Racing Union, which became the basis of the revised rules when the IYRU, and the NAYRU, agreed on a uniform code. He also was responsible, with some friends, for introducing Contract, as opposed to Auction, Bridge, to the card playing world.

Another great cup defender was Emil J. Mosbacher, who has twice defeated Australian challengers. In 1962 he took complete charge of Weatherly, while in 1967 he steered Intrepid. He would probably have become deeply involved in 1970, but at the time he was serving President Nixon as Chief of Protocol.

A very great British dinghy sailor, now well into his sixties, is Stewart H. Morris, whose name will always be associated with the International 14ft dinghy. He won the Prince of Wales Cup twelve times, over a period of 33 years. He won the Olympic Gold medal in the Swallow class in 1948 and his other racing successes are too numerous to mention.

He seems most at home in the Itchenor Sailing Club, where young dinghy sailors have hung on his every word for many years. Apart from his racing prowess, Morris has made a tremendous contribution to the organization of sailing in Britain, having served on the RYA council, Appeals Committee, Dinghy, Keelboat, General Purposes and Increased Scope committees at different times since 1935. He has also represented Britain on the IYRU.

Turning to the Offshore racing world, the outstanding British sailor of the postwar period has been Captain John H. Illingworth RN retd. His successes in Myth of Malham, which he designed in collaboration with J. Laurent Giles set British offshore racing on its modern way. More recently his success as a designer has been fantastic, with particular influence in France during the early 'sixties, when this aspect of the sport was really gaining strength across the Channel.

Having started here are more:

Designers

I have only heard of two men described as 'The greatest yacht designer in the world', although to be sure that title applied, during his lifetime, to Nathaniel B. Herreshoff, whose creations defeated the cup challengers at the turn of the century. He has been dead for many years, but the remarkable thing about this astonishingly talented man, was that he was an innovator. His memory lives on at Bristol, Rhode Island, where there is a small museum, kept by his son, Sydney. This contains many of the half models of the famous yachts which he designed and built.

Herreshoff never drew hull lines of his creations, preferring to carve half models himself and transferring the lines of the yacht direct, and full size, onto the floor of the mould loft. Students of yacht design should try to visit this museum, if only because they will find Herreshoff's version of almost everything that is considered 'new' in modern yachting. He flirted with catamaran design in the 1880s, but preoccupation with the design of torpedo boats for the US Navy prevented him from further development, until his dotage.

Britain's greatest yacht designer was certainly the late Charles E. Nicholson, who I have heard described as the World's greatest. Nicholson was responsible for four America's Cup challengers, two of which actually took two races off the defenders. The first was Shamrock IV, defeated by three races to two by Resolute. Shamrock V lost 4–0 to Enterprise, Endeavour 4–2 to Rainbow and Endeavour II, 4–0 to Ranger.

After the defeat of Endeavour, judged by most to have been the better boat, he presented her lines to Starling Burgess, Rainbow's designer. It was from these that Burgess and Olin Stephens developed Ranger, believed to have been the 'ultimate' in racing yacht design, of her time (1937).

Nicholson's talents were not confined to large sailing yachts. He designed many fine motor and steam yachts, as well as many racing boats of the metre classes. Two of his small one-designs are still racing, namely the Bembridge Redwing and the Lee-on-Solent Seagull. His family firm still prospers under the capable hands of his great-nephew, Peter Nicholson, who leads a design team which can still rival the world's best.

Olin and Rod Stephens first rose to fame with an ocean racer called Dorade. Since then they have certainly been the biggest influence on the world's yacht racing scene. As already mentioned, Olin, and Rod too, were involved with the design of Ranger. Since then they have designed the cup defenders Columbia, Constellation and Intrepid. They have also designed many of the world's great offshore racers, including nearly half of the fleet involved in the 1971 Admiral's Cup.

Apart from the 12 metre defenders, they produced many outstanding smaller boats of the metre classes, although strangely they never seemed quite happy with the 5.5. metre class. The Lightning is an example to show that they could also produce a popular centreboard boat, which has international status as a class.

Olin and Rod are both in their sixties and however long they live their influence on yacht design will remain, in the same way as that of Nat Herreshoff. They have rivals. Dick Carter has been making his mark, particularly in the offshore racing world in Europe. Britton Chance Jr. was rather surprisingly chosen to 'improve' Intrepid for her second America's Cup defence against

Gretel II, but he produced some superb 5.5 metres. Bob Derecktor seems to show a little spark of real genius every now and again, as has Charlie Morgan, Gary Mull, expatriate Englishman, Alan Gurney and sailmaker, Ted Hood.

Outside the USA, there is Cuthbertson and Cassian operating in Canada, while in Australia there is probably the finest potential successor to Olin Stephens in the shape of Alan Payne, as the world's greatest. It is a pity that there is not, at present, the yachting population, in his country to enable him to design yachts full time.

In Britain Nicholsons still produce really fine offshore racers. Angus Primrose, who was partner to Capt Illingworth, has yet really to prove himself, as has George McGruer, of the famous Clyde yachtbuilding family. Andre Mauric designed the French cup challenger France, and one always has the feeling that French flair may throw up a very great designer, particularly with their great interest in small cruiser/racers.

Turning to the dinghy world, I have already mentioned the work of Uffa Fox, Jack Holt, Ian Proctor and Peter Milne, whose boats have revolutionized dinghy sailing. Canadian Bruce Kirby, with his International 14 footers and the Laser, is making his own mark, while Bob Miller, who produced the Contender, is also in the Offshore racing and America's Cup business, has his chance to break through, as a rival to Payne in Australia.

Yachting administrators

The sailing world is governed by the IYRU. This friendly body holds its main meeting yearly in the Royal Thames Yacht Club, usually in November. The reason for the London meeting is that the Secretariat of the IYRU is the same as that of the RYA, English being the official language of yachting.

The Permanent Committee of the IYRU consists of delegates from various yachting regions, and while this body tends to be severely criticized in certain quarters, there is no doubt that there is a wealth of talent available.

Immediately after the war the President was Sir Ralph Gore, who, as the Commodore of the Royal Yacht Squadron, gave the

53

gathering a 'Grand Old English Gentleman' image. However, he was succeeded by Peter Markham (now Sir Peter) Scott, the artist, broadcaster, ornithologist, glider enthusiast and dinghy sailor. Scott was a close friend and rival of Stewart Morris in the international 14's and he won the Bronze medal in the Olympia-jolle at Kiel in the 1936 Olympic Regatta.

While Scott, who had a heartbreaking experience as the helmsman of the defeated America's Cup challenger Sovereign, was not really a great sailing competitor during his term of office at the IYRU, he was a truly great Chairman of meetings, and undoubtedly helped that body to face the future with some semblance of realism. Maybe they tended to try to introduce 'change for change's sake', but at least there was a fresh mind at the head.

Scott was relieved of the Presidency, by the very charming Italian yachtsman Dr Beppe Croce, from Yacht Club Italiano, Genoa. Croce is a sailor of great international experience, having sailed in centreboard boats and in the Stars before the war. He was in the Italian Six-metre at Torquay in 1948 and was Team Manager at Helsinki in 1952. He has the distinction of having owned five boats of the 5.5-metre class since 1952, so that he has an intimate knowledge of the kind of 'infighting' involved in class policy.

Beside Croce, at the meetings of this august body, sit two Kings, both Olympic Gold Medallists. King Olav V of Norway won his at the 1928 games in the 6-metre class, while exiled King Constantine of the Hellenes took the Dragon class at Naples in 1960, having trained with Paul Elvström.

Probably the strongest delegation on the IYRU is that from the NAYRU, led by Robert N. Bavier, himself the helmsman of Constellation when she defeated Sovereign in the America's Cup of 1964. Supported by Commodores Harry Morgan and George Hinman from the New York Yacht Club, as well as Harry Anderson (NAYRU Secretary) with Olin Stephens around for technical advice, this group tend to show up any British representatives as comparative 'lightweights, particularly since Stewart Morris has bowed out. Jonathan Janson, a member of the crew of the Royal Dragon Bluebottle, when she won the 1956 Olympic bronze, seems to show signs of redressing this balance, particularly now that he is Vice President of IYRU, but some decisions made in recent years seem to reflect a certain lack of British force.

However, one of those who has long been in the background at IYRU meetings, has been Gerald Sambrooke Sturgess, a retired Dental Surgeon, who is the greatest authority on the yacht racing rules in the world today. He has been on the IYRU Rules Committee since 1948 and his books and articles on the subject have been the 'gospel' for the racing sailor. His racing experience has been largely confined to the Norfolk Broads, where he owned one of the historic Norfolk Punt class, but as a Commodore of several

clubs up there, his experience of dealing with rule situations in racing in confined waters is unparalled.

On the fringe of the IYRU, but in the thick of an ever increasing sphere of yacht racing, has been Alan H. Paul recently retired as Secretary of the RORC, a post he had held since 1947. The club are still lucky enough to retain his help as Rear Commodore. After the war, when the RORC regrouped, having contributed a very large number of officers to the Royal Navy in 1939; (whether they were already professionals or amateurs at the time matters not) Paul was appointed with the terms of reference to the club as a 'Managing Director'.

His success is shown in the club's international influence and membership, and is reflected in the admiration with which its race organization is held all over the world. He has been succeeded as Secretary of the RORC by Mrs Mary Pera, herself an expert sailor and the author of one of the best books on celestial navigation ever written.

The modern competitive world girdlers

Joshua Slocum has been dead for many years, but his imitators live on, or have, like Sir Francis Chichester, followed him to calmer waters. The credit, or blame for the modern tendency to race across oceans or round-the-world single handed can be fairly placed upon the shoulders of H. G. 'Blondie' Hasler, who dreamed up the Single-handed Transatlantic race. Hasler was a very distinguished Royal Marine Officer, who was the actual hero of a wartime exploit, which was immortalized into a film called *Cockleshell Heroes*.

After the war he demonstrated how a 30-square metre could be sailed with a really resolute crew in offshore races. These boats were of very light displacement and regarded with suspicion by offshore sailors of 1947/48 vintage, but he proved that they could be driven hard.

It was however the 1960 Single-handed Transatlantic Race, which spurred Sir Francis Chichester to race against him. Hasler had done much research into the junk type rig for small yachts. He was also in the process of working on a self steering gear based on the Vane type, used by model yachts, but with a pendulum-servo assisted mechanism, which gave it greater power.

Sir Frances Chichester won that first race in 1960 and his books published later, notably *The Lonely Sea and the Sky*, give his background in great detail. He won the first of those races in Gipsy Moth III, which was a conventional offshore racer, designed by Robert Clark.

Whether or not the Single-handed Transatlantic Race has given yachting a boost, remains to be seen, but at least it has given designers of Single and multihulled craft a chance to experiment with complete freedom.

For the 1964 race there was a varied entry, with a very potent looking 44ft ketch called Pen Duick II, owned by Lieutenant Eric Tabarly of the French Navy, appearing as an obvious favourite to win, which he did, with Sir Francis second. Tabarly then took a third Pen Duick, a 57ft schooner, to win several offshore events including the Fastnet race.

The 1968 race was won by Geoffrey Williams, a schoolmaster, in Sir Thomas Lipton, with which he formed the nucleus of a fleet of new boats, which were built under his supervision for the Ocean Youth Club. As the name suggests, the boat was heavily sponsored, and Williams has had considerable success in finding sponsors for the OYC yachts.

The 1972 race produced several more heavily sponsored entries, notably the enormous Vendredi Treize, but in fact was won by Pen Duick V, a trimaran, sailed by Alain Colas, which had actually been designed for Tabarly for the 1968 race.

While this transatlantic race idea was gathering strength, Sir Francis, instead of sailing in the 1966 round Britain race, which was another of Hasler's brain children, set off on his epic voyage round the world. He was followed by Sir Alec Rose, then by Robin Knox Johnston, who did it in Suhaili, without stopping, in the *Sunday Times* race. Then came Sergeant Chay Blyth's epic voyage against the prevailing winds in British Steel, a heavily sponsored boat. Sir Alex Rose had intended to sail round at the same time as Sir Francis, but a series of disasters, which would have deterred anyone but this delightful man, who was a greengrocer as well as sailor, prevented him from doing so. His great humility has made him many friends. Sir Alec had no commercial support for his effort, although a few friends in his Langstom Harbour club helped him to buy a few new sails. Knox-Johnston was a seasoned voyager, having sailed Suhaili from Bombay before he set off round the world. He started in the *Sunday Times* race, almost before anyone realised he was off. It remains to be seen whether there is much more for the single-handed adventurer.

4 THE BOATS

In the first two chapters I gave some idea of the evolution of the sport and its different aspects. Now comes a chance to have a look at some of the craft which have become part of sailing history, or which are still making it.

In a book of this kind there is not enough room to list even a fraction of the number the types of boat and the various one-design classes which have lived and perhaps died. However, let us consider some of the boats which have graced the sailing scene in the modern world since the 1939–45 War.

The Olympic classes

The first postwar Olympic Games were held in England in 1948, and the sailing regatta was at Torquay.

The Classes which were sailed were: The 6-metre, Dragon, Star, Swallow and Firefly dinghy. It will be noted that all except the

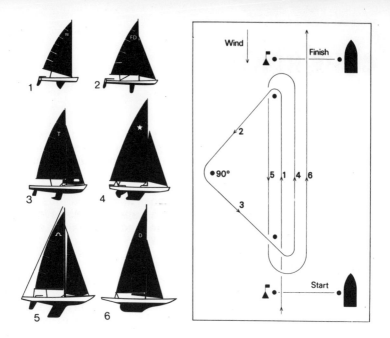

Firefly were keelboats. The 6-metre was sailed by five men, the Dragon by three, Star and Swallow by two and the Firefly single-handed.

The Six-metre, designed to the Metre-boat formula as shown in Chapter 2, could be variable in size, although the rules discouraged freaks, but an average sized boat of that period was LOA 37ft LWL 23.5ft Beam 6.2ft Draft 5ft. They carried about 460 sq ft of sail and they weighed about $4\frac{1}{4}$ tons, most of which was in the lead keel. Small wonder therefore that, despite the fact that they had been an Olympic class ever since sailing became an Olympic Games 'sport', they faded out after the 1952 Olympiad at Helsinki. Charles E. Nicholson, the great British designer labelled them 'potbellied leadmines', a name which was bound to stick, although he was not altogether unbiased, because at the time he was advocating a rule which eventually produced the 5.5 metre, of which more anon.

The Dragon was the result of a design competition organized by the R. Gothenburg YC (GKSS) in 1928, to produce an inexpensive young man's Cruiser/Racer for local waters. It has now grown to be an expensive boat, but still popular in many countries, 23 being represented at the 1972 Olympic regatta, at Kiel. The designer of this One-design boat was Johan Anker, of Norway.

Dimensions are: LOA 29.2ft LWL 18.7ft Beam 6.3ft Draft 3.9ft Sail area 267 sq ft. In order to reduce cost glass fibre construction is now permitted, as are metal masts. However, after sailing in every Olympics since 1948, the class was phased out at the 1972 meeting of the International Yacht Racing Union, who are responsible for such things.

The Star first appeared in 1911 designed by Francis Sweisguth, as one of the earliest build-it-yourself boats. It had been an Olympic class since 1932, but international interest seems to

Previous page: The Swallow class was in the 1948 Olympics, in which Stewart Morris won the Gold medal

Opposite left: Olympic boats at the 1972 Olympics. 1 Finn 2 Flying Dutchman 3 Tempest 4 Star 5 Soling 6 Dragon
Opposite right: The 1972 Olympic course at Kiel

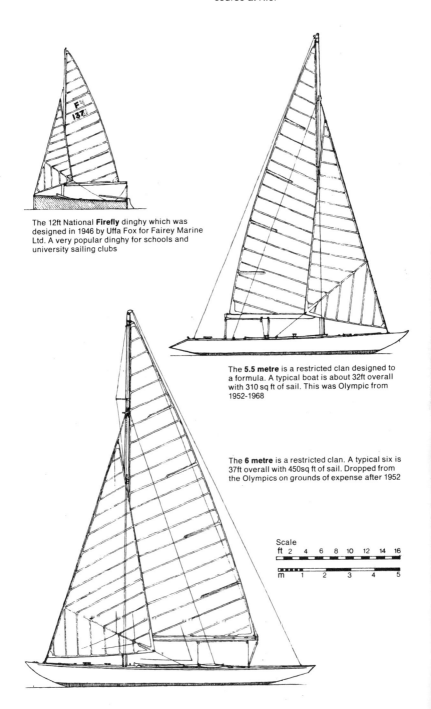

The 12ft National **Firefly** dinghy which was designed in 1946 by Uffa Fox for Fairey Marine Ltd. A very popular dinghy for schools and university sailing clubs

The **5.5 metre** is a restricted clan designed to a formula. A typical boat is about 32ft overall with 310 sq ft of sail. This was Olympic from 1952-1968

The **6 metre** is a restricted clan. A typical six is 37ft overall with 450sq ft of sail. Dropped from the Olympics on grounds of expense after 1952

Scale
ft 2   4   6   8   10   12   14   16

m   1   2   3   4   5

have waned slightly and it suffered the same fate as the Dragon at the hands of the IYRU, at the same meeting. The Star still has its addicts, although most of them sail in countries where there are light winds and warm water.

Dimensions: LOA 22.7ft LWL 19ft Beam 5.6ft Sail area 285 sq ft. A characteristic of this boat is that it carried no spinnaker, although as a rearguard action a Star did demonstrate one of these sails at Kiel at the Olympiad, too late to make any difference to the minds of the legislators.

The Swallow. This boat appeared in prototype form in 1946 in a competition to find a new British National two-man keelboat class. It was designed by Tom Thornycroft. It seems clear that the only reason why it became an Olympic class was the fact that it was suggested by the host country. It was a good boat, but not good enough to catch on, and never became an international class, adopted by the IYRU. Britain is the only country to have built any number, and it is sailed mainly by a crew of three.

Dimensions: LOA 25.5ft LWL 19ft Beam 5.6ft Draft 3.5ft Sail area 200 sq ft.

The Firefly was a 12ft dinghy designed by Uffa Fox, for hot moulded plywood construction by Fairey Marine Ltd, when they set up their plant for this type of construction after the war. It was really designed for two light people to sail and has become very popular among schools and universities.

Dimensions: LOA 12ft LWL 00ft Beam 4.6ft Sail area 90 sq ft.

This class was dropped from the 1952 Olympiad in favour of:

The Finn. This boat was the winner of a design competition promoted by the Finnish national authority to produce a suitable singlehander for the 1952 Helsinki Olympiad. It can be built of wood or glass fibre (nowadays) and it is remarkable in the cat boat rig (ie no headsail), with an unstayed mast, which revolves. It was far more the European idea of a singlehander than the Firefly and is comparatively heavy by modern racing dinghy standards. It has certainly stood the test of time and is still the Olympic single-hander for the 1976 games.

Dimensions: LOA 14.75ft Beam 4.9ft Sail area 114 sq ft.

As expected the Swallow was dropped from the 1952 Olympics, its place being taken by the

5.5 metre. This was to the formula which Charles E. Nicholson had advocated, although a draft restriction on the insistence of the Dutch, who only ever built one, spoiled it in the eyes of many. The 5.5 is sailed by a crew of three and a characteristic, which became a fashion, was the enormous spinnaker, often about 1,000 sq ft. The class remained Olympic until after the 1968 regatta at Acapulco, although it still has its addicts in the USA, Australia and on the Swiss lakes.

Dimensions of a typical 5.5 metre: LOA 32ft LWL 22ft Beam 6.4ft Draft 4.4ft Sail area 312 sq ft.

The Six metre having officially been given its death warrant by the IYRU, although it still lives, was dropped for the 1956 Melbourne Games. The Australians had many 12 sq metre sharpies in the country, a class which still flourished in Northern Europe.

The 12 sq Metre Sharpie is a long narrow hard chine centreboarder, with a gunter lug mainsail and a big overlapping jib. She is a tough boat to sail, but at least it was a step forward to have two centreboard boats in the Olympics, with three keel boats. Even in 1956 this hardly represented the balance of racing manpower in the world. The designer was J. Kroger.

The class is naturally nearly dying, replaced as it has been by other craft, but a lightweight version still flourishes in Australia.

Dimensions: LOA 19.6ft LWL 17.7ft Beam 4.6ft Sail area 130 sq ft. There was no spinnaker.

During the build-up for the 1956 Games another class was gathering strength, in the shape of the Flying Dutchman, designed by Uffa van Essen, as a new European lake class, but whose performance was found to be good enough in any conditions to be fully adopted by the IYRU as a truly international class. The FD had a deadly rival for Olympic honours, in the shape of the 505, which had been designed by John Westell, an Englishman, to replace the French Caneton. By somewhat devious means, when the rivals came up for the final judgement of the IYRU Permanent Committee, as to Olympic status for 1960, there was a *fait accompli*. The FD got selection without a vote, by that body. It had already been selected by the International Olympic Committee!

The Flying Dutchman soon spread, although maybe because it is a big long boat, so comparatively expensive, there are no really great numbers anywhere in the world. However, it has

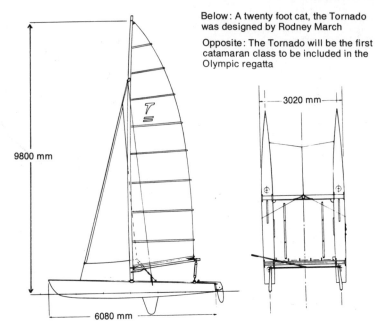

Below: A twenty foot cat, the Tornado was designed by Rodney March

Opposite: The Tornado will be the first catamaran class to be included in the Olympic regatta

9800 mm

3020 mm

6080 mm

drawn the elite of the small boat sailing world and is a far cry from one of its original design requirements. It had to be beamy enough to sleep one person each side of the centreboard case; and be stable enough for two to sleep on the same side.

With its beam it is quite an easy boat to sail, once one has got over its lightness and length, but it requires immense application to get the very best out of it.

Dimensions: LOA 19.8 Beam 5.9ft Sail area 180 sq ft.

The Olympic classes remained unchanged for the 1964 and 1968 Olympiads, but as already mentioned the 5.5 metre was dropped for the 1972 regatta. An attempt to displace the Dragon and Star in favour of the Tempest and Soling, which were conceived by the IRYU was defeated. However the Soling was chosen to replace the 5.5, while the Tempest got onto the 1972 list, when the number of Olympic classes was increased to six. Many felt that the imbalance of dinghy to keelboat was still ridiculous, but somehow the IYRU had to save face by adopting classes of their own conception.

The Tempest was designed by Ian Proctor as a two man keelboat, which might eventually replace the Star in the Olympics and in the sailing world as a whole. It is a planing keel boat not unlike a Flying Dutchman to look at, but with the crew using a trapeze and the extra stability given by the fin-and-bulb keel, she can carry her large sail and is an exciting boat in a breeze.

Dimensions: LOA 22ft Beam 6.5ft Draft 3.6ft Sail area 247 sq ft.

As already mentioned the Dragon and Star sailed in their last Olympic regatta at Kiel. The classes selected to sail in the 1976 games, the sailing part of which will be held at Kingston, Ontario, are: Soling, Tempest, Tornado Catamaran, Flying Dutchman, 470 and Finn.

This is a considerable step forward. The Tornado has proved
to be a very high performance catamaran indeed, with no op-
position from any other 'cat' class, although the very nature of its
high speed led to a certain amount of misgiving about how it
would fit in to the regatta pattern so far as courses were concerned.

The Tornado is a sloop rigged catamaran designed by an
Englishman, Rodney March. It is a strict one-design and was
already well established and very popular when adopted for the
Olympics.

Dimensions: LOA 20ft Beam 10ft Sail area 235 sq ft.

The 470 is a glass fibre dinghy of French origin, designed by
Andre Cornu. It was chosen in preference to the British Fireball
class, perhaps on the mistaken assumption that being a glass
fibre boat it would be more strictly one-design than the Fireball,
in which the hull material is optional. However it appeared that
there were doubts about measurement, and particularly hull
weight and strength, among many of those who were strange to
the boats, and who wanted to make up for lost time by buying one
immediately after Olympic adoption.

The boat looks rather like a smaller version of a Flying Dutchman, but can be sailed comfortably with a crew of total weight
about 22 stone. It has a spinnaker.

Dimensions: LOA 15.5ft Beam 5.5ft Sail area 137 sq ft.

Other dinghy classes

Having discussed the Olympic classes, it can be seen that a few
fell by the wayside, either because of price, obsolescence or they
never caught on.

As already mentioned in Chapter I, the **Snipe** has been an
International class for many years in fact, as well as a name.
Introduced in the US it has spread worldwide.

Dimensions: LOA 15.5 Beam 5ft Sail area 100 sq ft.

American sailors, although they have mostly been brought up
in their own local classes, tend nowadays to take note of the boats
which have been adopted by the IYRU. However there is one type,
which they evolved on their own, and which has caught on in the
most remarkable fashion, particularly where the water is warm
enough. This is the 'sailing surfboard' typified by the Sunfish and
Sailfish classes, of which the total numbers of the two reach up
into hundreds of thousands. No doubt, with this in view, the new
Laser has been introduced as something a little more soph-
isticated.

Dimensions of Sailfish: LOA 13.7ft Beam 2.95ft sail area 75 sq
ft, Cat rigged.

Another class which originated in the USA, but which has
spread worldwide, particularly after it caught on in Scandinavia,
is the **Optimist** pram dinghy, which is just about the cheapest and

easiest boat to build. This is a children's class but the boats are frequently sailed by parents.

Dimensions: LOA 8ft Beam 3.5ft Sail area 35 sq ft.

Keel boat classes

Despite the reduction in the number of keelboat classes in the Olympic Games, there are still a very great many of these classes in existence all over the world. I have mentioned the demise of the Six-metre, or its supposed demise in the eyes of the IYRU, but on the Western seaboard of the USA the class is very much alive.

In recent years there was a revival of the Eight-metres in Scottish waters, while once again several are still in commission in the USA, Australia, Canada and Scandinavia. There are even some of these graceful boats in the Mediterranean.

The Twelve-metres spring to life whenever an America's Cup looms up and some of these boats have been ocean raced successfully, such as Ted Turner's American Eagle, or converted into fine cruising yachts.

It seems doubtful whether the Dragon will suffer much from its non-Olympic status. Many feel that it will still spread, particularly in local fleets, if only because owners who are keen, will return to the fold and not trek round continents in the hope of gaining experience and qualifying for the Olympics.

It will be interesting to see whether the Etchells 22, which is now adopted as an International class, as many thought it should have been in preference to the Soling, will flourish.

The comparative dimensions are:

Soling LOA 26.75ft Beam 6.25ft Draft 4.25ft Sail area 233 sq ft. Designed by Jan Linge, Norway.

Etchells 22 LOA 30.5ft Beam 6.97ft Draft 4.5ft Sail area 316 sq ft. Designed by E. W. Etchells.

The offshore racers

The early offshore racers were usually cruising craft, which in turn had been evolved from the typical working boats. A very particular example is shown by Jolie Brise, winner of the first and two other Fastnet races. She was a converted Le Havre pilot boat, built in 1913. Her main dimensions were, LOA 56ft LWL 48ft Beam 15 ft 9in Draft 10ft 2in Sail area 2,400 sq ft. Before the very first Fastnet doubts were expressed on the suitability of such small craft for offshore racing.

One of the most significant yachts in the list of winners of the Fastnet (see appendix), is Dorade 52ft OA, the first offshore racer from the board of Olin Stephens. Her success brought fame to her designer and to his brother Rod, who has helped him so much with the rigging, and the mysterious rites known as 'tuning' the fine vessels to Olin's design.

Another significant yacht, also to Olin's design, was the $38\frac{1}{2}$ft

OA Centreboard yawl Finisterre, owned by Carleton Mitchell. She won the Bermuda Race three times running. Mitchell has said that 'There was only one Finisterre', although there were some near sisters. However, she was magnificently sailed by a superb skipper and crew, and she was of a type which was an example of the best boats produced by the Cruising Club of America rating rule.

In England just after World War II, one of the greatest trend setters was Capt John Illingworth's 39ft OA Myth of Malham, with her comparatively light displacement, short ends and hogged looking sheerline. For a time Nicholsons ruled the roost, but inevitably the offshore racing fleet on both sides of the Atlantic became dominated by Olin Stephens. A few designers are pressing him, with an occasional good boat, well sailed, but he appears to be head and shoulders above the rest of the world. Why else would a British Prime Minister go to him for his first three big yachts?

A recent development in the offshore racing world, has been the desire of some owners to race level, or maybe for some clubs to encourage level racing. This was contrary to the old concept of offshore racing, when the idea of the handicap rules was to try to level existing craft, of differing sizes shapes and rigs. Now IOR Mark III is being used for levelling out racing amongst offshore racing type boats.

The first blow in this movement was struck by the Cercle de la Voile de Paris, with their International Cup. This had, for many years been called the 'One Ton Cup', only because it was originally for competition for a class whose keel weight was restricted to One Ton. It was switched from this class to the 6.5 metre class and then to the Six-metres, who last sailed for it in 1963. The CVP then decided to put it in contention amongst offshore racing type boats. Nowadays the IOR rating limit for the One ton cup contest, is 27.5 rating.

As a result of this rejuvenated competition, there are now classes for the Two Ton Cup, the $\frac{3}{4}$-ton cup, the $\frac{1}{2}$-ton cup and the $\frac{1}{4}$-ton cup. Needless to say none of these competition requirements

Two vintage gaff-rigged yachts, typical
of the cruising craft of many years ago.
These were probably conversions, or
based on the design of working boats

have anything to do with tonnage, in any way.

The $\frac{1}{2}$-ton and $\frac{1}{4}$-ton Cup size of boat has developed greatly in recent years because of the influence of the British Junior Offshore Group and the American Midget Offshore Racing Club, both of which have encouraged offshore racing in boats which were too small to be admitted to the races organized by the 'elders' of the RORC and the Cruising Club of America.

Cruising yachts

On both sides of the Atlantic, early cruising yachts followed working craft lines and were none the worse for it, except for the fact that the owners forgot what the working craft were designed for. Some sailed best with a full cargo, eg, of fish, so that they floated too high without the cargo. Other fishing boat types were designed, like the Brixham Trawler, with low freeboard so that the fishermen could handle nets. In consequence they had too little headroom below, unless their topsides were built up. Many found that converted racing boats made fine fast cruisers, but they often inherited all the faults and few of the virtues of the racing boat.

Small cruisers of the 'twenties and 'thirties tended to have poor headroom, if they were to sail at all well and probably had an inadequate auxiliary engine, if indeed the diehard owner would have one at all. Many a fine engine installation in a pre-war yacht suffered dismally from complete neglect and disuse. Our fathers and grandfathers tended not to have to hurry back to the office.

Nowadays, one has only to glance through such publications as *Bristow's Book of Sailing Cruisers*, or in the USA, *Sailboat and Sailboat Equipment Directory*, to see the infinite variety of craft available. Some are 'ready made' offshore racers, while some have no pretension at speed under sail. However, what they have is COMFORT. Whether they are beautiful specially built yawls or ketches; offshore racers overtaken by modern standards of discomfort, or the floating caravan; whether single hull, or multihull, twin keel or single fin keel, they are almost without exception, designed with at least the modicum of comfort and some with great luxuries. This is the age, so far as the cruising man is concerned, of comfort. The boat is probably the answer to the country cottage, and, as mentioned before, the womenfolk will not go sailing unless they have their creature comforts.

The excellence of the modern cruising yacht is due in part to the development of the modern offshore racer. It is possible, however, that with increased international competition the modern offshore racer is being reduced to a spartan shell, in which the accommodation is sacrificed on account of weight, as is the really essential requirement of feeding the crew adequately, if they are to give of their best.

5 THE YACHTING CENTRES

'The Yachting Capital of the World' title has been claimed by Newport, Rhode Island, although the yachting fraternity, who frequent Cowes Isle of Wight, would probably dispute this.

Since the first post-war America's Cup series at Newport in 1958, the town went into a considerable decline, if only because of the rundown of the US Navy base. Thames Street, Newport's answer to Cowes High Street, looked depressed, and while the big houses on the Ocean Drive came to life with the Australian invasion of 1962, the town itself looked unhappy. By 1970, however, the Newport Preservation Society were in action and many of the fine old houses near the waterfront were saved from destruction, and a new bridge across Narragansett Bay, helped to bring tourism into the town.

Cowes has long been a ship building port, although the importance of this has tended to be ignored by yachtsmen. It is more industrial in its nature than Newport, which explains the reluctance of the local council to do anything to encourage yachtsmen to go there at all, until quite recently. Now, with the yearly invasion of an enormous number of offshore racing yachts, particularly in the odd numbered years with the Fastnet race and Admiral's Cup series, facilities for visiting yachtsmen and their

boats have become top priority.

Since the Royal Yacht Squadron started, and perhaps even more importantly, Queen Victoria installed herself at Osborne House, Cowes became important to those who went yachting, with a capital 'Y'. Her relatives, the Tsar and the Kaiser visited. So did Louis Napoleon, hoping for support.

Newport, with its imitation European great houses, built slightly later than the days when Cowes first became fashionable, was the rendezvous for all that was great and gracious on the American yachting scene. The surnames of many of those who frequented both Cowes and Newport are still often identical. It was, perhaps a question of which branch of the family was helping which, whether it was with a title to a noble house, or some much needed finance.

The Royal Yacht Squadron is the centre of the traditional Cowes regatta week, which is always held between Goodwood horse racing week, and the Twelfth of August, when it is legally possible to shoot Grouse. The British Social calendar is inflexible in these matters. In 1948 the Olympic Games were held in England, There was no question of the date of Cowes Week, which clashed with the Olympic Regatta, at Torquay, being changed. One

Previous page left: Part of the
waterfront at Newport, Rhode Island—
America's most famous yachting centre

Previous page right: Beating along
Cowes Green, where 'People of
condition' took to sailing early in the
nineteenth century

suspects that much the same rules apply to the dates of the New
York Yacht Club cruise, in which Newport plays a very important
part.

While we can riducule this apparent phenomenon, there are
other regattas which have become traditional. Many who are newcomers to sailing organization, tend to ignore these fixtures. For
many years there has been a sailing regatta at Cannes during the
last week of January. It is now Ski/Yachting, with a break on the
slopes for those who need diversion from sailing. Not long ago
golf was included in the programme, although one suspects that
with decreased holiday time among modern sailors this has
become impracticable.

Genoa regatta has always been held in late February or early
March. Sometimes the weather is wintry, but that is its slot in the
programme. Yacht Club Italiano has its headquarters at Genoa,
although many members find Portofino more agreeable. Naples
was the host for the 1960 Olympic Regatta, but the sailing fraternity in Italy are thin. At Easter time, San Remo has become the
venue for the Olympic classes, although Cannes, and more
recently Hyeres has claimed support.

From the Mediterranean there is a switch to northern Europe
as the weather improves. Kiel Week, the regattas at Copenhagen,
Hanko, Marstrand (or Lysekyll) and Sandham have their well
established claims. Helsinki is perhaps slightly off the beaten
track, as is the Clyde, whose Fortnight regatta was always the first
two weeks of July. Cowes Week, as mentioned, is permanent, but
the French hold Deauville and Le Havre dear to them.

In the south of England, it was customary for those who still
sailed in mid August, to 'bend on tanned canvas and sail down
west'. What better than the relaxed fun of the West country.

Of course there are clashes of dates, even the most traditional
ones. Holland Week, Menai Strait Week and West Highland Week
are at the same time as Cowes. The recent British Olympic Training regatta, which has been held in Poole Bay since 1961 and
which takes place at the end of May or early June, tends to clash
with Kiel week. It is now to be moved to Weymouth Bay, for better,
one hopes.

In the USA the opening of the year brings a large offshore racing
fleet to Florida, for the Southern Ocean Racing Conference series
of races. This takes a fleet of more than a hundred of the finest
ocean racers, many of them the very latest, to St Petersburg and
during the course of the series, to Fort Lauderdale, Miami and
Nassau, in the Bahamas. After a couple of visits to this yachting
festival one is struck by the continual growth of the sport and the
improvement of facilities. Indeed, those who have forced their
ideas on a municipality, to improve their marina facilities, have
often been under heavy pressure from obstructionist elements,
who can see no point in their scheme at all. A year or two later the
same obstructionists are blaming those with the pioneering spirit
for lack of foresight. The facilities are simply not big enough.

National Tourist Boards, or whatever they may be called, have
discovered yachting in a big way. In underdeveloped regions
such as the West Indies the yacht charter business grows con-
tinually. A pioneer in this field was Commander Victor Nicholson,
who set up in English Harbour, Antigua, which he discovered
almost by chance. His set-up set the pattern for many other
charter operators in the Caribbean, where, a year or two ago,
there was a serious decline because of the dollar crisis. However,
the West Indies has its great charm, particularly for the American
yachtsman, for winter diversion.

The start of the annual Sydney-Hobart
race, which is always on Boxing Day

Flying over the coast of the USA one is struck by the incredible
amount of navigable water, which is still unused and where peace
can be found. Americans are gregarious people and their boating
folk are no exceptions. The vast fleets of boats in the favourite
yachting ports on the West Coast, leave visitors from Britain completely flabbergasted. The scale of marina operations in Florida
make the Hamble River look comparatively small.

The waters of Long Island Sound, which is the US equivalent to
the Solent, but more crowded, boasts some fine yachting ports,
pride of which must be Oyster Bay, home of the famous Sea-
wanhaka Corinthian YC, one of the earliest clubs to encourage
'corinthianism'.

In Australia yachting is rapidly developing into a major sport.
It always was popular, but with improved communication with the
rest of the world, the wide horizons of international competition
are in sight, and Australia is becoming one of the greatest
yachting countries. Sydney, Melbourne and Perth will soon rival
the great yachting ports of Britain and America. The Sydney-
Hobart race is already a yachting classic.

In New Zealand, sailing and Rugby are the topics of conversa-
tion rivalling golf in Britain. Auckland certainly rivals Cowes as
one of the great sailing centres of the world.

In the Mediterranean, as already mentioned, the South of
France and Italy have long been on the established 'circuit'. However the delights of the Balearic Islands have drawn many from
North Europe who seek the sun and warmth. Spain is increasingly
tourist conscious, so that marina development is in full swing.
Greece is another country where yachting as a tourist attraction
is being encouraged. As a cruising ground the Greek Islands rival
the Caribbean and the yacht harbours of Piraeus, with the Royal
Hellenic Yacht Club standing guard, are full of many of the finest
yachts to be found in the world.

6 WATCHING A YACHT RACE

A yacht race can be extremely confusing to watch for the layman. A sailing regatta can be even more confusing, because the different classes often mingle with each other.

Yacht racing throughout the world is governed by a code of rules, which are provided by the International Yacht Racing Union, which in some respects can be amplified or slightly modified by the national authority. In Britain the national authority is the Royal Yachting Association, while in the USA it is the North American Yacht Racing Union.

For each race there are the sailing instructions, which are part of the rules, which set out such essentials as the description of the starting and finishing lines, the course, the time(s) of the start(s), any time limit etc. They may also include a list of entries. This will invariably be the case in big regattas, in which such information as the sail numbers of the competitors will also be given.

There are two main ways of marking the starting line. The first, as can be seen on page 30, is by means of transit posts on shore, usually at the club running the race. There is then a mark buoy to show the outer limit of the line, although in narrow rivers or estuaries the line may stretch right across and there may be another set of transit marks. The sailing instructions will indicate how the boats are told which way they should go. This is sometimes by a simple big arrow.

The other main type of line is an imaginary one laid from a committee boat, as on page 30. This is between a committee boat, the mast, or some prescribed point on the boat, being one end, the other being a mark buoy laid far enough away to allow the competitors to get across the line at the same time without ramming each other. They sometimes do in any case. This latter type of line is laid for the Olympic-type course. In this case the first leg of the course will be dead into the wind, so that the boats will be tacking after the start.

Obviously, therefore, the thing to avoid, if you are in a spectator boat, is getting in the way. For a starting line such as in A, keep well behind the line, or to the side of it if there is room. For B, keep behind or well to the side.

A yacht race is started by signals from the committee boat or signal station by two different methods; the first used mainly in Britain and the second in America. These are:

Warning signal	Class flag broken out	White shape
Preparatory signal	Code flag P (Blue Peter) broken out	Blue shape
Start	Both flags lowered	Red shape

In the second system each shape is lowered 30 seconds before

Rescue, from the left: 'Man overboard!' The skipper is about to gybe round so that. . . . He comes up head to wind with no way on. If there is a ladder the man can be helped up it, but if there is not. . . . He can be hauled up on one of the halyards

the next is hoisted. When a regatta is started one class after the other, the start of one class can be the warning or preparatory signal for the next. The intervals between the signals are usually five minutes, but this will be shown on the sailing instructions.

Attention is drawn to the signals by a gun or other sound signal, eg bell or hooter.

If a yacht is over the line prematurely, a second gun will be fired (or hooter sounded) immediately after the starting gun. If a great number of boats are over, which cannot be recalled individually, or cannot be identified, then there is a *general recall*, the sound signal being two guns (Code flag First substitute, a blue triangular flag with blue border).

A premature starter returning to the line must return and recross it correctly, and while she is so doing she has no right of way over those which have started correctly.

Basic racing rules
After the Preparatory signal the boats have to comply with the yacht racing rules. Very simply these are governed by four fundamental rules:

A port tack yacht shall keep clear of a starboard tack yacht.

A windward yacht shall keep clear of a leeward yacht.

A yacht clear astern shall keep clear of a yacht clear ahead.

A yacht which establishes an overlap to leeward from clear astern shall allow the windward yacht ample room and opportunity to keep clear, and during the existence of that overlap the leeward yacht shall not sail above her proper course. (ie course to next mark).

Naturally there are other rules, which apply to situations such

as overtaking, rounding marks and approaching obstructions and such like. The rules in the full text are always available from national authorities, while there are many explanatory books on the subject, as well as magazine articles.

Spectator boats

I have already mentioned keeping clear of the starting line and the same applies to the finishing line. The finish can be very close, so it is essential never to be in a position which might prejudice the chances of any competitor. Never park yourself on the finishing line, not that the committee would let you. If up to windward, keep well up to windward, if the boats are tacking up to the finish.

Again, during the actual race keep well clear to *leeward* of all marks of the course. Keep well clear to leeward of all competitors. There is a tendency for keen photographers to creep up to leeward of their favourite boat to take a shot, but the presence of a motor boat close-to can ruin a helmsman's concentration, so you may be doing your favourite a lot of harm.

Wakes of motor boats are also irritating, particularly in calm weather, when rocking will ruin the set of the sails and help to stop a sailing boat.

Rescue

It sometimes happens that spectators find themselves having to try to rescue the crew of a boat which has capsized, or go to the aid of a dismasted boat. It is one of the customs of the sea to go to the rescue of those in peril, but ask them if they need help before barging in. Most modern dinghies are designed to be easily rightable, but crews can get tired, particularly if the water is cold.

Remember, if you are in a motor boat, that a capsized boat may have lines trailing round it. You will not want to get any of these round your propellor. With a capsized dinghy get hold of the top of the mast. If you are picking a man up, do so from the bow, or amidships, *never over the stern*, where there is danger from a turning propellor, which can be lethal. If a man in the water gets anywhere near the prop, you must stop it.

Anyone who goes aboard any boat should have an idea of 'man overboard' drill. Look to see where the lifebelt is stowed and how to release it. If a man falls overboard, or if picking up a number of people, have someone to watch them.

The pictures show the correct way of rounding up to rescue a man overboard. Remember that his hands will be slippery and he may not be able to grip.

Handicap races
Many races are sailed under handicap, so that different types of boats can all race together. In this case the usual practice is for them all to start together and the handicap is applied by some Time Correction at the end.

There are different systems of handicapping. For offshore racers there is a system of Rating, whereby various hull and sail measurements are taken and the formula in force, eg the International Offshore Rating Rule Mark III, is applied to find the Rating. Length in a sailing yacht is speed, and the higher the rating the higher the theoretical speed.

From the rating it is possible to calculate what is known as the Time Correction factor, and the Basic Speed Figure.

The Time Correction Factor is the figure which is multiplied by a yacht's Elapsed Time (time taken to sail the course) to find the Corrected Time, on which prizes are given. This was the system used by the RORC until 1973.

The Basic speed figure is the yacht's theoretical time in seconds to sail a mile. Therefore, if the Time-on-distance system of handicapping is used (as in USA), it is possible to calculate the theoretical time each boat should take to sail the course. You can therefore arrive at this for every competitor and handicap them accordingly. The advantage of this system is that you know your handicap before you begin.

In England in 1973 the RORC were trying out a new system, under which the elapsed time to sail the course, the yacht's rating and the length of the course are all taken into account.

For small yachts and dinghies, for which measurements for rating would be a ridiculous expense, there is the Portsmouth Yardstick method of handicapping. Each type of boat has a Portsmouth Number given to it after years of observation. Eg 78 for a Flying Dutchman and 93 for a Snipe. To get corrected time one divides the elapsed time by the Portsmouth number, over 100.

7 CRUISING CLUBS, ASSOCIATIONS AND SAILING SCHOOLS

Cruising clubs

The first Cruising Club to be formed in the world was undoubtedly the Water Club, of Cork Harbour, now the Royal Cork YC. In 1720, when it was formed, the members of the Water Club made little or no effort to race each other. Their main pleasure was to cruise around in company with naval type manoeuvres, and join up for conviviality at sundown.

To celebrate the 250th birthday of the Water Club, there was a great gathering of yachts in Cork Harbour. The Cruising Club of America organized a transatlantic race, in 1969, to finish at Cork. The Royal Cruising Club arranged for as many members' yachts as possible to rendezvous there, as did the Irish Cruising Club. The fact that it was a year earlier than the birthday they celebrated mattered little. Celebrations of the real birthday year could be left to the racing men.

A fleet of nearly a hundred yachts then cruised in company along the south west coast of Ireland, stopping off for a couple of days at each port for a celebration, organized by each of the clubs in turn. It is said that a British retired admiral managed to persuade the Irish Army to erect the marquee for the RCC party, as a military exercise.

The Royal Cruising Club was founded in 1880, mainly through the influence of Sir Arthur Underhill, who was its Commodore

Previous page: Where organized
yachting began, an old print of the
River Lee showing Blackrock Castle,
Cork

The Clyde Cruising Club organizes
several 'musters' during the season

from 1886 till 1936. It was to be a strictly cruising body, organizing
no racing. The membership was limited to 300 people of either
sex, with a cadet membership of 25, for young men and women
between 18 and 25. The club 'meets' at various ports, and in winter
there is a periodical dinner party, which have an informal air
about them. The club publishes an annual book with the cruises
of its members for all who are interested to read. Prizes are
awarded for meritorious cruises and a 'Seamanship Medal' is
presented to a person of any nationality who, in the opinion of the
judges, has performed an outstanding act of seamanship.

The RCC is connected to the Cruising Club of America in a way,
which can best be described as 'avuncular'. It was in 1921 that
William Washbourn Nutting, Casey Baldwin and James Dorsett
sailed across to England in a gaff rigged ketch called Typhoon, a
boat which is described in Uffa Fox's first book. The idea was to
sail to England to arrive at Cowes for the Harmsworth Trophy
motor boat race, which indeed they did.

It was at Cowes that Nutting and his friends met that pillar of the
RCC, Claud Worth, whose Yacht Cruising was a classic of its day.
As a result of conversations between these two Nutting dreamt

St George's Grenada, a popular winter
rendezvous for members of the
Cruising Club of America

up the idea of forming the Cruising Club of America. On his return
a meeting was convened at 'Beefsteak John's' in Greenwich
Village. This was followed by a meeting at the Harvard Club when
the 36 charter members duly formed the club, which has, ever
since performed the combined functions of both RCC and RORC.

Meanwhile other cruising clubs were formed. The Cruising
Association, which has the finest yachting library in London was
founded in 1908 and has a wider membership and slightly wider
scope than the RCC.

In 1909 the Clyde Cruising Club was formed at Rothesay, where
the fleet still 'muster' annually. The CCC is unique among cruising
clubs in that it has a cadet dinghy section which has sailed for
many years at Bardowie Loch. This club does in fact organize
races and is doing a lot to encourage offshore racing in the Clyde
area, this side of the sport having been somewhat neglected in
Scotland. In common with many other cruising clubs, the Clyde
Cruising Club publish a very excellent book of Sailing Directions
for the West Coast of Scotland.

The Irish Cruising Club was formed in 1929 and here again we
find that they publish sailing directions for parts of the Irish Coast.

They have their annual dinner at Cork, Dublin and Belfast in rotation, although it is understood that recently this routine has been broken because of the troubles in the north.

One of the newer cruising clubs is the Cruising Yacht Club of Australia, which seems to follow the pattern of the Cruising Club of America, in that it is the organizing body for offshore racing. It is this body who sponsors the Australian team for the Admiral's Cup.

The Little Ship Club is another predominently cruising organization, with a fine clubhouse looking over the River Thames in the heart of the City of London.

All these clubs have one main thing in common, and that is the training in seamanship of their members. This is the most important thing and a really unique organization is the Island Cruising Club, with its headquarters at Salcombe in South Devon. As well as running courses for beginners, in dinghies, the club owns a number of large cruising yachts, which are maintained very largely by volunteers. They are crewed up on a rota system and have sailed far and wide.

In these days very few individuals can afford big boats, but the ISC has these and thus gives many hundreds of its members a chance to sail in a yacht many of them will probably never be able to afford. Membership, for the complete beginner is easier, because this club will consider candidates on references from their professional advisers, eg Lawyer, or Bank manager.

For some clubs there is a seagoing qualification and some readers may have noticed men wearing a tie with a flying fish motif on it. This is the emblem of the Ocean Cruising Club, which was formed in 1954. The distance qualification is a non-stop voyage of more than a thousand miles, so that a passage from the UK to Gibraltar would be sufficient qualification. Colin and Rosemary Mudie qualified with a voyage, which started in a balloon, which came down in an attempt thus to cross the Atlantic!

Sailing schools
Having dealt with the subject of cruising clubs, the complete beginner may still find difficulty in starting to sail. However, in Britain and indeed all over the world, there are schools which will teach the beginner to start sailing.

The whole subject of training for beginners is very much in the minds of the Royal Yachting Association, because of their continual fight to keep the sport as free of government restriction as possible. The RYA does inspect sailing schools in this country to ensure that they maintain a sufficiently high standard. The Sports Council run courses in sailing in both England and Scotland as well, but if the beginner has any doubts in his mind at all those at the RYA, at 5 Buckingham Gate, London, will advise them. They will probably also recruit them as members of that body.

GLOSSARY

Aback When the wind is on the wrong side of the sails

Abaft Behind, aft of, eg abaft the mast—behind the mast

Abeam Abreast, or at right angles to the centre line

About Go about, or tack

Accommodation The domestic part of a yacht, eg sleeping and living quarters

Adrift Broken away, not under control. Also sailors expression for being late

Aft Towards the back, or stern

Ahead In front

A'lee In a leeward direction, eg 'Hard a'lee', 'Helm a'lee', when tiller put down to leeward on tacking

Aloft Above the deck

Amidships Line across the middle of ship between stem (or bow) and stern

Astern Behind

Athwart Across

Aweigh When 'Anchor's aweigh', it is clear of the bottom

Backing Of wind, means it is going anticlockwise, or against the sun in the northern hemisphere. Of sails. Hauling clews of sails to windward. *See* clews

Bail Taking the water out with an open container, bucket, can, or bailer

Ballast Weight to help stability and counterbalance the effect of wind on sails

Bare Poles No sails up

Batten To batten is to fasten hatches, portholes securely. A batten. A thin slat of wood or plastic to help a sail set better

Beam The width at the widest part, and a transverse piece of wood or metal supporting the deck

Beam ends A ship flung on her side is on her beam ends

Bear Away Sail away from the wind

Bear down on To steer towards

Bear off Steer away from wind

Bear up Steer closer to wind

Beating Sailing to windward as much as possible. *See* tacking

Beaufort Scale Numerical notation of wind velocity. *See* appendix

Belay To secure with figure of eight turns round belaying pin, cleat or bollard

Bend Type of knot for joining ropes

Bilge The curve between side and bottom of boat, or the extreme bottom of the boat where water collects

Block Pulley. 'Two blocks' means that two pulley blocks have been pulled tight together

Bollard A post for securing mooring lines

Boom A spar to stretch out the lower edge of a sail

Bowse Haul or tighten

Bowsprit Spar projecting from bow

Breast rope Mooring rope leading abreast to jetty, dock or another boat

Broad Reach Wind abaft the beam, point of sailing between reaching and running

Bunk boards Boards, or canvas screens to keep occupant from falling out of bunk in rough weather, or when yacht is heeled over

Buoy A buoy to which a ship may be moored, or a navigational aid moored to indicate a position

Burgee A swallow tailed flag (Naval), or a triangular distinguishing flag of a yacht club

Cable Measure of distance, 200 yards (100 fathoms). Rope or chain of anchor

Check To stop. Or with a sheet or halyard, to ease out slowly

Cleat Two armed hook of wood or metal for securing ropes

Clew The corner at the rear end of a sail, where the leech joins the foot

Closehauled Sailing as close to the wind as possible

Close reefed All reefs down

Compass Navigational instrument pointing to the north. Lives sometimes in Binnacle.

Course Angle made by ships track to a meridian

Crutch Fork for holding up boom, when sails not set. Naval term for rowlock

Dingy Small open boat. May be yacht's tender

Doghouse Raised part at aft end of cabin

Dog vane Wisp of cloth on shroud to tell wind direction, sometimes called 'tell tale'

Downhaul Rope for pulling things down

Down helm Put tiller down to leeward

Dowse Take in sail, or lower spars quickly

Draught The depth of water required to float a ship, or the belly in a sail

Earrings Light rope or line which hold a sail to a spar, eg reef earrings.

Ease To luff for seas or strong winds. Of rope, check, or let go slowly

Ensign National flag flown or 'worn' by ships

Fairleads Metal or wood guides for ropes or chain to prevent chafing and improve the lead of a rope or chain easing friction

Fall The part of a rope on which you pull

Fend To push off. Hence Fenders, Fendoffs, which are pads to protect a ship's side

Fitting-out To overhaul a ship after a lay up eg for winter

Flake To flake is to coil a rope so that it can run out readily

Flare A light signal. Or, in design, the concave upward curve of a ship's bow

Foot Lowest edge of a sail

Fore Front

Fore-reaching When going about, luffing or hove-to, a boat will carry her way into the eye of the wind. This is fore-reaching

Foresail Sail set on principal forestay

Free Sailing free is to have the wind between close-hauled and aft

Freeboard Distance between deck and waterline

Full A sail which is drawing well. Sometimes 'A good full'

Full and by Sailing to windward close-hauled with a 'good full'

Furl To gather a sail to its spar, or stay and lash it. There is 'roller furling', by which this is done by rotating a spar or stay

Gaff A spar at the head or top of a four cornered sail

Gash Rubbish, eg Gashbucket

Gear Masts, sails, cordage, winches etc above deck, or crew's clothing, bedding etc

Gimbals System by which compass, stove etc may be suspended at sea to keep surface horizontal

Gooseneck The hinge between the boom, or other spar and the mast

Goosewinged Setting the headsail with its clew the opposite side to the mainsail when running before the wind

Gunwhale The top edge of an open boat

Guy Controlling rope on a spar (eg Main brace in square rigged ships). Controls the windward edge of spinnaker, ie is attached to the boom. In Scotland known as spinnaker brace

Gybe Bringing the wind from one side to the other by passing stern on to it

Halyard A rope used for hoisting sails, flags, or even yards

Hand, to Bring in sails, by lowering, furling

Handsomely Gently, slowly

Hanks Clips for attaching sails to stays

Harden in Pull sails in

Haul wind Sail closer

Head Fore end of ship. Marine toilet so-called because it was situated in bow or head of ship. Draughty. Also top corner of triangular sail

Headsails Sails forward of mast

Heave to To take way off, or stop, keeping close to head to wind or sea

Helm down To put tiller down to leeward, so ship's head to windward.

Helm up, opposite to helm down

Hitch Method of securing rope to any object eg Clove hitch

Hoist Pull up

House flag Owner's private signal

Horse Bar or wire athwart a boat on which a block travels

Hurricane *See* Beaufort Scale

Irons A boat is in irons if she is head to wind and will not answer helm, ie cannot be steered

Jib The foremost headsail. Genoa jib, special overlapping jib, led abaft the mast

Jury Makeshift. International J—adjudicate on protests in international regattas

Kedge Light anchor for temporary use. To kedge is to move a boat by hauling up on anchor, anchoring again and repeating process

Keel Lowest part of boat on fore and aft line

Kicking Strap A line or tackle from

boom to heel of mast to stop boom rising

Knot A nautical mile per hour

Lazy With a rope means an extra one eg sheet or guy

Lead Weight on end of rope (leadline) to measure depth of water or the angle of a sheet and the fitting the sheet is led through

Leading edge Forward edge

Lee Away from wind. Sheltered side

Lee-bowing Sailing a boat so that tide or current catches the lee bow and pushes boat to windward. Tactically tacking under an opponent's lee bow, to give him dirty wind

Leech After edge of a sail

Lee-Oh Helmsman's expression when he is putting helm down to tack. (Keep your head down)

Let Fly Let go sheets

Lift Rope to take weight of a spar eg Topping lift of mainboom, or spinnaker boom

Limber holes Holes in floors and between ribs of boat to let water flow to lowest part of bilge

LOA Length of a boat overall

Log Instrument to measure speed through water

Logbook Ship's diary

Loom Handle of an oar, or glow of a lighthouse (ship) in the sky before the light itself is visible

Lubber's point This is fixed on a compass to show where the ship's head is pointing

Luff To luff is to bring the head of a boat closer to the wind. Of a sail, is the leading edge

LWL Load Waterline, on which vessel floats, if at her designed weight

Make Sail Hoist the sails

Mast The vertical spars on which sails are set, or to which spars are attached. M-step. Socket in which heel or bottom end of mast sits

Midships As a helm order, put helm on centre line

Moor To lie to a mooring, or to more than one anchor

Multihull Vessel with more than one hull, eg Catamaran, trimaran

Neaps Tides with least rise and fall.

Neaped is when a boat goes aground on falling tide and the next tide will not provide sufficient water for her to float off

Off the wind Point of sailing, not close hauled

On the wind Closehauled

Outhaul Eg A clew outhaul is the rope or wire which pulls the clew out

Overhaul To catch up another craft. To slacken off a rope. To pull apart the blocks of a tackle

Painter A rope used for mooring up a dinghy, bow or stern

Part Of a tackle, can be the standing part or running part. To P-, to break

Partners The supports where a mast goes through a deck

Pay off To let the boats head to swing away from the wind, so that the sails will fill

Pay out Slacken a rope under control

Pennant, or Pendant A short piece of rope. Or a triangular flag

Pinching Sailing too close to the wind

Pintles Metal pins on a rudder which pivot in the gudgeons

Pointing How close the boat will sail to the wind

Points, reef Light bits of line for tying up a reefed part of a sail

Pooped When seas overtake a vessel running before the wind and sea and fall aboard

Port Left hand side facing forward. P-Tack, wind from port side

Pram Dinghy with a transom at each end

Pulpit Railings round bow of boat. Stern pulpit sometimes known as pushpit

Punt Vessel used on rivers, but sometimes applied to small dinghy

Quarter Between the beam and the stern. Q-berth is the bunk under the side of the cockpit

Rake Angle off the vertical of a boat's mast

Reach Sailing with wind free, but dead aft

Ready about Warning that helmsman is about to tack

Reef To shorten sail

Reeve Pass ropes, eg sheets, through any fitting

Rhumb Line A straight line on a Mercator's projection chart

Riding Light All round white light which should be shown in fore rigging when at anchor

Rig The arrangement of masts, sails and rigging. To rig is to get these set up

Roach Curved edge to the trailing edge of a sail

Roller reefing Shortening sail by rolling sail round a spar, eg the main boom

Round turn A complete turn eg of a rope round a bollard

Rowlocks Gaps in the gunwhale of a boat for pivoting the oars. Sometimes used for metal or plastic crutches

Rubbing Strake Piece of wood or plastic outside boats hull to prevent damage from rubbing

Rudder Board or plate which directs the ship

Runner Detachable backstay which is eased away so that main boom can be squared off. R-winches set up the runners

Running Sailing with the wind aft, further aft than broad reaching

Samson post The main mooring post of a ship

Scope The mount of cable let out when at anchor

Set Flying A sail not attached to a stay

Shackle A D shaped fitting for attaching sails to sheets, halyards etc

Sheets Ropes used to control the set of sails

Shrouds The wires holding up the mast in a lateral plane

Snub To check suddenly

Soldier's Wind Fair wind, without tacking either there or back

Sound To find the depth of water, eg Echo Sounder, otherwise referred to as Depthmeter

Spar A solid piece of wood or metal on which a sail is set

Spill To spill is to empty a sail of wind

Spinnaker Sail with three edges which is set on the opposite side from the mainsail when running or broad reaching

Springs Mooring ropes running from forward on boat to aft on shore or vice versa. Also highest and lowest tides

Stanchion Pillar. Or posts for lifelines

Starboard Right hand side looking forward. Starboard tack, wind on starboard side

Start To ease, ie let go under control

Stays Wires supporting mast in fore and aft direction

Steerage way Enough speed for the rudder to work

Stem The timber or plate at the very forward end of the vessel. To stem, is to meet the tide, current etc

Stern The back end

Stops Pieces of rotten yarn or rubber bands for holding a sail in control close to its luff

Strop A band of rope or metal

Strum Box A box with holes, fitted at the suction end of the pipe from a bilge pump to prevent shavings, paper etc clogging it

Swig Take a pull on a halyard at right angles to it to make it tauter

Tabernacle The step which hinges for a mast which can be lowered

Tabling Nautical term for the hem of a sail

Tack The lower forward corner of a sail. A leg or board, when beating to windward. To tack is to alter course from port tack to starboard or vice versa, with bow through the wind

Tackle. Pronounced Taickle. A combination of blocks and rope forming a purchase

Thimble Grooved metal or plastic ring which lines an eye in a rope to prevent wear

Throat The upper corner nearest mast of a gaff sail

Thwarts Seats in a small boat on which the rower(s) sit

Transom Square part of the after end of a vessel

Trim Adjust sails with the sheets. Or the horizontal equilibrium of a vessel. Trimmed by the stern means she is down by the stern

Under Way Not attached in any way to mother earth

Unship Remove

Vang A rope controlling the end of a gaff or sprit. Also to control a spinnaker or main boom

Veer The wind veers when it follows

the sun in a clockwise direction in the Northern hemisphere

Warp A rope by which a vessel is moved, eg to warp

Wear To alter course from one tack to the other stern on to the wind

Weather helm A vessel carries weather helm if it is necessary to keep the helm to weather to steer a straight course

Weigh To get the anchor up

Withie A light stick or post to mark the navigable channel of a small creek or river

Yaw To swing about off course, by bad steering or bad sail trim

Further Reading

General

Creagh-Osborne, R.
Dinghy Building, London 1963

Harle, P.
Glenans Sailing Manual, London 1963, New York 1967

Knights, J.
Sailing Step by Step

Lane, C. D.
The New Boatman's Manual, New York 1962, London 1967

Phillips-Birt, D. (ed.)
Yachting World Handbook, London 1967

Sleightholme, J. D.
ABC for Yachtsmen, London 1965, New York 1965

Encyclopedia of Sailing, New York 1971

Knots

Day, C. L.
Art of Knotting and Splicing, London 1964, New York 1970

Spencer, C. L.
Knots, Splices and Fancy Work, Glasgow 1956

Weather

Coles, K. A.
Heavy Weather Sailing, London 1967

Watts, W. H.
Weather for Yachtsmen, London 1964

Offshore Racing

Davies, M.
Australian Ocean Racing, Australia 1962

Illingworth, J. H.
Further Offshore, London 1969, New York 1969

Loomis, A.
Ocean Racing, London 1936

Parkinson, A.
Nowhere is too far, New York 1960

Phillips-Birt, D.
British Ocean Racing, London 1960

For Seawives

Morrison, Felice,
Gourmet in the Galley, London 1969, New York 1971

Sleightholme, Joyce,
The Sea Wife's Handbook, London 1970, Chicago 1971

Racing

Elvstrom, P.
Paul Elvstrom Explains, London 1965

Elvstrom, P.
Expert Dinghy Racing, London 1963

Proctor, I.
Racing Dinghy Handling, London 1962

RYA Publication
Yacht Racing, London 1969

Sturgess, G. S.
Yacht Racing Management, London 1961

White, R. & Fisher, B.
Catamaran Racing, London 1968, New York 1969

Ocean Voyaging

Gerbault, A.
Fight of the Firecrest, London 1955, New York 1955

Slocum, J.
Sailing Alone Around the World, New York 1954, London 1968

Robinson, W. A.
Deep Water & Shoal

Uffa Fox's pre-war 'Annuals'

Sailing, Seamanship and Yacht Construction, London 1934

Uffa Fox's Second Book, London 1935

Sail and Power, London 1936

Racing Cruising and Design, London 1937

Thoughts on Yachts and Yachting, London 1938

Periodicals

British
Yachting World
Yachting Monthly
Yachts and Yachting
Yachting and Boating Weekly
Boat News
Practical Boat Owner

American
Motor Boat and Yachting
Yachting
Boating
Motor Boating
Sail
Rudder
Yacht Racing

8 APPENDICES

The Beaufort Wind Scale

Beaufort number	Description	Speed in knots	Metres/second
0	Calm	Less than 1	0.0
1	Light Airs	2	1.5
2	Light breeze	5	3.0
3	Gentle breeze	9	4.9
4	Moderate breeze	13	6.9
5	Fresh breeze	18	9.0
6	Strong breeze	24	10.8
7	Moderate Gale	30	13.0
8	Fresh Gale	37	—
9	Strong Gale	44	—
10	Whole gale	51	—
11	Storm	60	—
12	Hurricane	70+	—

Olympic scoring system as used at Kiel Olympic regatta 1972
1 There shall be seven races for each class of which the best six for each yacht shall be counted for her total points. When six races only are sailed the best five for each yacht shall be counted for her total points.
When five races only are sailed all five shall be counted.
2 Each yacht which finishes in a race shall score points as follows:

First place	0
Second place	3
Third place	5.7
Fourth place	8
Fifth place	10
Sixth place	11.7
Seventh place and below	Place plus six

The Royal Yachting Association rules that a yacht which ranks as a starter and does not finish, including a yacht which infringes the rules but retires within a reasonable time, shall score points for a last place finish, ie for the finishing place equal to the number of starters.

A yacht not retiring within a reasonable time, or which is disqualified gets points for last place, plus ten per cent of the number of starters.

A yacht which did not start gets points for finishing place competitors (an entrant who has started in any race of the series).

For a short series the RYA recommends the following: First place 3/4 points, Second Place 2 points, Third place 3 points etc.

Newport to Bermuda Race Winners

Although there were several races before the first war, the present Newport RI to Bermuda class was first sailed in 1923. Since 1924 it has been sailed in alternate years. Nowadays it alternates with the Fastnet race.

The fastest time was made by Bolero, the 73ft yawl, then owned by Sven Salen, of Sweden. She took 70 hours, 11 minutes, 40 seconds over the 635 mile course. Winners overall on corrected time have been:

1923 Malabar IV, schooner, owner, John Alden
1924 Memory, yawl, R. N. Bavier
1926 Malabar VII, schooner, John Alden
1928 Rugosa II, yawl, Russell Grinnell
1930 Malay, schooner, R. W. Ferris
1932 Malabar X, schooner, R. I. Gale & John Alden
1934 Edlu, sloop, R. J. Schaefer
1936 Kirawan, cutter, R. P. Baruch
1946 Gesture, sloop, A. H. Fuller
1948 Baruna, yawl, Henry C. Taylor
1950 Argyll, yawl, William T. Moore
1952 Carina, yawl, Richard Nye
1954 Malay, yawl, D. D. Strohmeier
1956 Finisterre, yawl, Carleton Mitchell
1958 Finisterre, yawl, Carleton Mitchell
1960 Finisterre, yawl, Carleton Mitchell
1962 Nina, schooner, DeCoursey Fales
1964 Burgoo, yawl, Milton Ernstof
1966 Thunderbird, sloop, Vincent Learson
1968 Robin, yawl, Frederick Hood
1970 Carina, sloop, Richard Nye
1972 Noryema, sloop, R. Amey (Great Britain)

Admiral's Cup Winning Teams

1957 Great Britain
1959 Great Britain
1961 United States
1963 Great Britain
1965 Great Britain
1967 Australia
1969 United States
1971 Great Britain

The Fastnet Race

The course is nowadays from Cowes, round the Fastnet Rock and back to Plymouth. The distance is officially given as 605 miles.

The fastest time was made by Ted Turner's ex-Twelve metre American Eagle, whose elapsed time was 3 days, 7 hours, 11 mins., 48 secs.

Winners on corrected time, British, unless otherwise stated were:

1925	Jolie Brise	Cutter	Lt. Comdr. E. G. Martin
1926	Ilex	Yawl	Royal Engineer YC
1927	Tally Ho	Cutter	Lord Stalbridge
1928	Nina (USA)	Schooner	Paul Hammond, Elihu Root and DeCoursey Fales
1929 1930	Jolie Brise	Cutter	Lt. Comdr. E. G. Martin and Robert Somerset
1931 1933	Dorade (USA)	Yawl	Olin and Roderick Stephens
1935	Stormy Weather (USA)	Yawl	P. Le Boutillier
1937	Zeearend (Holland)	Yawl	C. Bruynzeel
1939	Bloodhound (USA)	Yawl	I. Bell
1947	Myth of Malham	Cutter	Captain J. H. Illingworth RN
1949	Myth of Malham	Cutter	Captain J. H. Illingworth RN

1951	Yeoman	Sloop	Owen Aisher
1953	Favona	Sloop	Sir Michael Newton
1955	Carina II (USA)	Yawl	Richard Nye
1957	Carina II (USA)	Yawl	Richard Nye
1959	Anitra (Sweden)	Yawl	Sven Hansen
1961	Zwerver (Holland)	Sloop	W. Van Der Vorm
1963	Clarion of Wight	Sloop	D. Boyer
1965	Rabbit (USA)	Sloop	R. Carter
1967	Pen Duick III (France)	Schooner	E. Tabarly
1969	Red Rooster (USA)	Sloop	R. Carter
1971	Ragamuffin (Australia)	Sloop	S. Fischer

The America's Cup

Once known as the £100 Cup of the Royal Yacht Squadron. Contrary to general belief the club challenges for this elusive cup, not the country. New York YC defend.

The Cup was won by the Schooner America in a race round the Isle of Wight, (approx 58 miles) beating 15 of the best British yachts. Challenges for the cup have resulted as follows:

1870	Magic	beat Cambria	R. Thames YC	1 race
1871	Columbia	beat Livonia	R. Harwich YC	2 races
	Sappho	beat Livonia		2 races
1876	Madeleine	beat Countess of Dufferin	R. Canadian YC	2 races
1881	Mischief	beat Atlanta	Bay of Quinte YC	2 races
1885	Puritan	beat Genesta	Royal Yacht Squadron	2 races
1886	Mayflower	beat Galatea	Royal Northern YC	2 races
1887	Volunteer	beat Thistle	R. Clyde YC	2 races
1893	Vigilant	beat Valkyrie II	Royal Yacht Squadron	3 races
1895	Defender	beat Valkyrie III	Royal Yacht Squadron	3 races
1899	Columbia	beat Shamrock	R. Ulster YC	3 races
1901	Columbia	beat Shamrock II	R. Ulster YC	3 races
1903	Reliance	beat Shamrock III	R. Ulster YC	3 races
1920	Resolute	beat Shamrock IV	R. Ulster YC	3 races to 2
1930	Enterprise	beat Shamrock V	R. Ulster YC	4 races
1934	Rainbow	beat Endeavour	Royal Yacht Squadron	4 races to 2
1937	Ranger	beat Endeavour II	Royal Yacht Squadron	4 races
1958	Columbia	beat Sceptre	Royal Yacht Squadron	4 races
1962	Weatherly	beat Gretel	R. Sydney YS	4 races to 1
1964	Constellation	beat Sovereign	R. Thames YC	4 races
1967	Intrepid	beat Dame Pattie	R. Sydney YS	4 races
1970	Intrepid	beat Gretel II	R. Sydney YS	4 races to 1
1974	The NYYC face challenges from France and Australia, Great Britain and Canada having withdrawn.			

Index continued from page 93

INDEX

93